Born to
SHOP

F R A N C E

Third Edition

Born to
SHOP
FRANCE

Third Edition

SUZY GERSHMAN
and
JUDITH THOMAS

Introduction by
FRED HAYMAN

BANTAM BOOKS
TORONTO • NEW YORK • LONDON
SYDNEY • AUCKLAND

TO OUR HUSBANDS

Although every effort was made to ensure the accuracy of prices appearing in this book, it should be kept in mind that with inflation and a fluctuating rate of exchange, prices will vary. Dollar estimations of prices were made based on the following rate of exchange: 5.5 French francs = $1 U.S.

BORN TO SHOP: FRANCE
A Bantam Book / April 1986
Bantam Second Edition / April 1987
Bantam Third Edition / February 1989

Produced by Ink Projects

Library of Congress Cataloging-in-Publication Data

Gershman, Suzy.
  Born to shop. France / Suzy Gershman and Judith Thomas.—
3rd ed., Bantam 3rd ed.
    p.   cm.
  Includes index.
  ISBN 0-553-34602-4 (pbk.) : $7.95
  1. Shopping—France—Guide-books.   I. Thomas, Judith
(Judith Thomas) II. Title.
TX337.F8G47   189
380.1'45'0002544—dc19   88-15066
                                                                                        CIP

Published simultaneously in the United States and Canada

Bantam Books are published by Bantam Books, a division of Bantam Doubleday Dell Publishing Group, Inc. Its trademark, consisting of the words "Bantam Books" and the portrayal of a rooster, is Registered in U.S. Patent and Trademark Office and in other countries. Marca Registrada. Bantam Books, 666 Fifth Avenue, New York, New York 10103.

PRINTED IN THE UNITED STATES OF AMERICA

FG   0 9 8 7 6 5 4 3 2 1

The BORN TO SHOP Team:

reported by:
Suzy Gershman
Judith Thomas
original reporters of first edition:
Suszette Gallant
Suzy Kalter Gershman
Carolyn Schneider
Judith Thomas
Paris correspondent: Pascale-Agnes Renaud
editor: Jill Parsons
executive editor: Toni Burbank
assistant to executive editor: Ellen Powell
cover design: Krystyna Skalski
cover art: Dave Calver
text design: Lynne Arany
copy editor: Archie Hobson
maps by: Judith Thomas and Lauren Dong

Acknowledgments

This is the part where we thank everyone who helped us get it together for this new edition. So hugs and kisses and great big thank-yous all around to: Bantam Books and the *Born to Shop* team, who really worked hard in order to accommodate all the changes we made from the last edition to this one; Bruno Ferté and Jean Claude Lopez de Ayora, from the Hôtel Meurice in Paris, and the staff of the Meurice, who always go out of their way to help us do our work.... Marli, we miss you at the Meurice; Michelle Oaklun of Loew's Hotels; Jacques Bacon for his hotel savvy and Doctor S. S. Kalter, who helped us test all the other *"Born to Shop"* hotels"; Jean Pierre Tournai, our primary contact in the French cosmetics business, who always fills us in on the latest and the greatest in new fragrances and keeps us up-to-date on changes in and secrets of this special business; Debra C. Kalter, the famous Doctor Debbie, who works for us in London and who flew into Paris with us a few times to help out; and Pascale-Agnes Renaud, our Paris correspondent, who helped us take on the South of France in great style.

CONTENTS

Introduction

I have known the authors of this book for several years now. They come into my store on a regular basis.

They touch all the clothes.

They write down some prices in little leather notebooks they think I haven't noticed.

They smile a lot.

They never buy.

So you can imagine my shock when one day I spied one of them at the bar, sipping a Perrier and waiting for her package to be wrapped. Was it perhaps a gift?

No, she said, she was buying a few odds and ends to wear on her next trip to Europe. I knew she went to Europe often—after all, in Beverly Hills everyone knows everything about everyone else. I also knew she bought most of her clothes in Europe. Then we fell into a deep discussion about the real reason for all her trips to Europe. She was writing a book about retailing. We got so chummy just standing there chatting that I wasn't at all surprised when she asked me to write the introduction to the book. After all, we at Giorgio's certainly know a few things about retailing.

The book arrived at my office and I discovered it was about retailing, all right ... about *discount* shopping for some of the very same names we had made famous on Rodeo Drive.

Surprise turned to outrage. I wondered, just for a minute, if these women were trying to put me out of business. Then I relaxed and began to laugh. I realized they are geniuses.

This book gives the reader a full dose of inside information that I have never before seen explained to a person outside of the business. Even *Scruples* didn't explain the nitty-gritty this well. The secrets of how international retailing actually works are revealed in these pages, and with them is the formula for getting the most for your money.

So I applaud these women on their hard work and excellent book. And I wonder if, now that I've written the introduction to this book for free, I will get the name of the place where they got those fabulous fake Cartier necklaces.

Fred Hayman

Preface

Voilà! Or *voici*! Or something like that. Here it is, friends, the latest edition of *Born to Shop: France.* Toss out your old edition, or put it away as a collector's item. You have in your hands the new, updated version. Not only have all the old listings been rechecked, but we've added more listings, and our last chapter, a complete shopping tour of the South of France, is brand-new.

We also give you more of what's special about Paris, and all of France; more of what is affordable; and more of what makes sense as a smart buy. We have plenty of designer listings, as always, but we've whittled down our information on the couture, and we don't list every Benetton in Paris.

We've added information about hotels. We have some snack and shop tips; some heretofore never published secrets about saving money on getting there; and *métro* stops to help you find your way once you've arrived. So stick with us; if you were born to shop, we've got plenty to share with you.

We prepared this revision with tender loving care, with the usual rules:

▼ The stores we visit have no idea who we are—all shopping and reporting is done anonymously.

▼ No store can buy a listing in this book or any other book we write.

▼ We visit each shop again before a revision, so each listing in this book has been visited recently, and probably visited twice.

▼ All opinions expressed are our own—this is a very opinionated book. Any guidebook can simply list the stores and markets of Paris. We go out of our way to use our professional judgment to tell you the best way to organize your time in order to maximize your shopping pleasure.

▼ These books are updated and revised regularly, but if you catch a change before we do, please drop us a card or a note:

Born to Shop
Bantam Books
666 Fifth Avenue, 25th floor
New York, NY 10103

And yes, we will try to answer your letters personally. But please, no more phone calls at home in the middle of the night.

Suzy Gershman and Judith Thomas

1 ▾ THE SHOPPING EXPERIENCE

Shopping in France

One spin around the Place de la Concorde at night and you'll know why Paris has been dubbed the City of Light. After shopping there over the years, however, we find Paris leaves us light in the head with all that style per metric foot; light in the pocketbook from all the bargains; and light on the scale after doing mile after mile (excuse us—kilometer after kilometer) of shopping, shopping, shopping.

Paris is one of the world's premier shopping cities. Even people who hate to go shopping enjoy it in Paris. What's not to like? The couture? The open markets? The most extravagant kids' shops in the world? Jewelers nestled together in shimmering elegance? Perfumes and cosmetics at a fraction of their U.S. cost? Antiques and collectibles that literally are the envy of kings? It's just not hard to go wild with glee at your good luck and good sense for having chosen such a place to visit.

Paris also is a very simple city to shop once you know what you're doing. It's all logistics—Paris is a large city, and there's soooo much of it to conquer. While most of the glamorous boutiques are clustered in about four distinct and not-that-far-apart neighborhoods, when you get to the real bargains, you need to do a bit of traveling. (One of our favorite shops isn't even inside Paris; it's in a suburb called Clamart—and it's difficult to get there by public transportation.) Unless you have scads of time on your hands, you'll find your shopping time in Paris involves making choices and rating priorities. You'll always be sorry you didn't

1

get to one neighborhood or another; but you'll always have an excuse for returning to the City of Light. No matter how little you have time for, you'll still have no trouble spending your budget.

Wherever you go in France, you find style—from the street markets where fresh produce is piled high, where the flowers beg you to buy them, to the stores and secret *passages* of the Paris streets. Barge through the country, take your bike, buy a new pair of walking shoes—France is waiting for you to discover her one more time. And her shopkeepers are standing by, calling your name.

Be Prepared

We thought we left homework behind the day we graduated. But the bargains go to the shopper who is ready to recognize them, and that means doing some homework.

▼ If you have favorite designers or targets of acquisition for your trip, shop the major department stores and U.S.-based boutiques (if in your city) for comparison prices. Don't assume you will get a bargain on a European purchase.

▼ If you do not live in a city that has a lot of European merchandise, do some shopping through *Vogue* and *Harper's Bazaar*. In the ads for the designer boutiques, you'll find phone numbers. Call and ask about prices and sales. Don't be afraid to explain that you are contemplating a shopping trip to Europe and are doing some comparison pricing.

▼ Read French magazines to get familiar with looks, shops, and life-styles. They cost a fortune (sometimes $14 a magazine), but many libraries have these magazines; go to a French hairstylist just to read them.

▼ Or go in with several friends on a foreign magazine co-op. You may want to get a subscription to the French *Vogue* and share it among four other friends. Or buy an issue of *Passion. Passion* is a tabloid newspaper published in France about life in Paris. The good news: It's totally in English and extraordinarily hip!

▼ Understand the licensing process. Two men's suits may bear the identical label—of a well-known French designer—but will fit entirely differently because they are made entirely differently.

▼ French cosmetics and fragrances can be extraordinarily less expensive in France, or so marginally less that it doesn't pay to schlepp them home. You'll save 30% to 40% on Chanel makeup but only 10% on Lancôme. Homework will pay off here.

▼ Don't be fooled by foreign-sounding names and think the merchandise with these names is cheaper in Europe. Because Americans are so taken by European names, many American-made products have foreign names.

▼ The best buys in France are on French designer merchandise that is on sale, costs enough to qualify for the *détaxe*, and fits into your suitcase and your U.S. Customs allowance; once over your $1,400 Customs allowance, you will pay 33% duty on those French bargains.

If you shopped in France in the dollar's glory days, you may be shocked at the current high price of French merchandise. Everything is expensive, even cheap merchandise. You may do enough homework to consider a splurge in a major American city at the designer sales rather than the cost of airfare and hotels. Don't go expecting bargains without understanding where the bargains are. Know your stuff before you go!

The Moscow Rule of Shopping

T he Moscow Rule of Shopping is one of our most basic shopping rules and has nothing to do with shopping in Moscow, so please pay attention. Now: The average shopper, in his pursuit of the ideal bargain, does not buy an item he wants when he first sees it, because he's not convinced that he won't find it elsewhere for less money. He wants to see everything available, then return for the purchase of choice. This is a rather normal thought process. If you live in an Iron Curtain country, however, you know that you must buy something the minute you see it because if you hesitate—it will be gone. Hence the title of our international law: the Moscow Rule of Shopping.

When you are on a trip, you probably will not have the time to compare prices and then return to a certain shop; you will never be able to backtrack cities, and even if you could, the item might be gone by the time you got back, anyway. What to do? The same thing they do in Moscow: Buy it when you see it, with the understanding that you may never see it again. But, since you are not shopping in Moscow and you may see it again, weigh these questions carefully before you go ahead:

1. Is this a touristy type of item that I am bound to find all over town?

2. Is this an item I can't live without, even if I am overpaying?

3. Is this a reputable shop, and can I trust what they tell me about the availability of such items?

4. Is the quality of this particular item so spectacular that it is unlikely it could be matched at this price?

If you have good reason to buy it when you see it, do so.

CAVEAT: The Moscow Rule of Shopping breaks down if you are an antiques or bric-a-brac shopper, since you never know if you can find another of an old or used item, if you can find it in the same condition, or if the price will be higher or lower. It's very hard to price collectibles, so consider doing a lot of shopping for an item before you buy anything. This is easy in Paris, where there are a zillion markets that sell much the same type of merchandise in the collectibles area. At a certain point you just have to buy what you love.

The Dollar and the Donut

Before we get into all our insider's information about Paris and the South of France, we do have something very important to tell you. When the dollar is not strong, there may not be many items that you can truly save money on. In fact, you may be surprised to find that sale prices in the United States on French merchandise can be better than the regular French prices on the same or similar merchandise. In some cases, the prices have actually been balanced by the manufacturer so that the same items retail for more or less the same price everywhere in the world. Don't go rushing off to France thinking that anything with a "Made in France" label is going to be cheaper. When the dollar is not particularly strong, your savings on some items may resemble a donut: a great big zero.

Best Buys of France

S ure you can hark back to those days when one dollar was equal to ten French francs, and you can moan and groan all you want. We call that negative thinking. Instead, we ask you to remember back when the dollar was equal to four francs, which is where the equation stood for years and years. (If you are not old enough to remember, you'll just have to trust us, but back in the dark ages when we made our first trips to France, the franc really was equal to a quarter.) Now that you've re-adjusted your thinking, things aren't looking so bad, are they? It's all a matter of perspective!

Yes, the price of our hotel room at the Meurice has gone steadily up; yes, a cup of coffee or a Coca-Cola at the hotel is outrageously expensive. But we ask you to remember a couple of very important tricks—you can beat the system. We insist on our dose of luxury hotel, but we save money by:

▼ Buying our own Cokes and mineral water at the grocery store and keeping them in the minibar. Every chic Frenchwoman in Europe carries a large tote bag with a 1.5 liter plastic bottle of her favorite mineral water.

▼ Buying food from fresh markets (one of France's most beautiful natural resources), from supermarkets, and *traiteurs* who sell ready-cooked gourmet meals—hot or cold. You can eat a fabulous French meal for $5 this way.

▼ Doing gift shopping either in duty-frees or at markets, open-air or of the *hypermarché* variety. You can find great deals on small giftables in Inno, Prisunic, or Auchan ... or in *métro* stops.

▼ Knowing prices at home, before going wild in Paris. There seems to be no rule as to where the savings are or aren't (except for cosmetics—see page 147). If you live in New York, or are spending time in New York before you go to Europe, please stop by Dollar Bill's (99 East 42 Street—it's adjacent to Grand Central Station), where we have seen many French and Italian designer buys (especially men's ties) at prices far lower than they are in Europe—even on sale in Europe! Also consider doing some shopping on the airplane as you fly back and forth. Get the price list on the way over, save it, and keep it handy for comparison shopping; then do the big buying on the trip home. Although airline prices for the same merchandise vary from carrier to carrier, you can expect excellent prices on Hermès scarves and Cartier watches. We think you'll do better on fragrance from a shop like Catherine (see page 150), but if you need a last-minute gift, the airline price will certainly be less than the U.S. department store price.

We can tell you about walking the streets of Paris depressed out of our minds that the prices are so high, bemoaning the fact that perhaps we would buy nothing, and then—on the same day—finding an Ungaro Sollo Donna dress for $100 on sale and a pair of woven leather shoes for $40 at a secret shoe source we have. Yes, some prices can be offensively high. But take heart. A bargain may be waiting for you just around the corner. Maybe the days of the mad shopping spree are over, but there are savings and good buys in Paris and in the South. Honest.

So, what should you buy in France? This list can vary from season to season, of course, but the places where we look for savings are:

In Paris:

▼ perfumes and cosmetics
▼ Bottega Veneta, if you find something you love in the sale niche downstairs
▼ Rodier (savings can be 30% to 40%)
▼ designer goods that qualify for the *détaxe* refund, so that we are guaranteed at least a 15% saving over the U.S. price just by getting the tax back
▼ pillowcases (antique linen and market specials)

In the South:

▼ pottery
▼ *faux* fragrances
▼ giftables from markets

Booking Paris/1

Y ou'll have no trouble finding guidebooks to Paris, but we do have two fabulous secret sources that we think you'll find indispensable. The first is *Paris Pas Cher* by Françoise and Bernard Delthill, published by MA Editions. This is a French guide written for French locals. Some years it is translated into English and sold in the United States, but it has not been popular here, so you may not find it. Buy the French edition (if you can read French, that is), which comes out in December of each year for the next year, at any bookstore in Paris. The authors have been writing this book for almost ten years and are cult heroes to Parisian locals. What they provide is an encyclopedia of listings of discount everything—from cheap eats to factory outlets. If they think the store is really a great find, they put a picture of a foot next to it (representing a French expression meaning "It's the cat's meow," but literally meaning something more like "It's the feet"). If you cannot read French, you can look for the feet and write down those addresses. We must announce that we do not always agree with the Delthills' opinion, and we have not been to every listing in their book, but you may find this a useful guidebook—especially if you are going to be in Paris for a long time and don't mind bombing out a few times. Shopper's note: The authors send out stickers of feet to the stores that are so recommended; don't be surprised to walk into a store and see a foot displayed in the window. In the United States, order the book from the Yale Co-op, New Haven, Connecticut.

You need absolutely no knowledge of French to read a little book called *Paris par Arrondissement*. Several publishers put out this book, in various sizes and bindings, because it is as essential as a *London A to Z* is in London— this is the book with all the streets, the maps, the bus and *métro* lines. Our edition, which fits into the palm, is so complete that you can look up an address in the front of the book and a chart will tell you the *métro* stop for your destination. You don't even have to look at the detailed neighborhood maps or the big foldout map. Our version is published by Editions L'Indispensable and actually has some instructions for use in English as well as French. We bought it at the Hachette at Opéra and highly recommend it.

Don't forget the newspaper *Passion*, which is also in English but reports on life in Paris. You can get a one year subscription to *Passion* for $40 or purchase a single issue at a newsstand for $5. For a subscription write to Paris *Passion*, 23 Rue Yves Tondic, Paris, France, 75010.

Booking Paris/2

When it comes to hotels in Paris, we have lots of information and two styles of doing business. Obviously, there are many hotels in Paris, many different prices, and various locations. We like to stay in the 1er *arrondissement* (see page 53), and have found three hotels, about a block from each other, that are all first-rate and very elegant at three different prices. We rate hotels as inexpensive (under $100 per night); moderate ($100–$150 per night); and expensive (over $150 per night). We think these three are all you need to know about hotels in Paris, but since you probably don't agree, we've brought in our expert Jacques de Larsay (see page 11). Our choices:

HÔTEL MEURICE: Frankly, we hardly ever stay anywhere else. The Meurice is small and quiet but drop-dead elegant, with the perfect location on the Rue de Rivoli—you can walk to shops everywhere, several *métro* stops are out the door, and you can pretend to be rich and famous, at least while you stay here. Because the Meurice is an Inter•Continental hotel, you qualify for any special promotional prices Inter•Continental may be offering, as well as several shopping discount services. Expensive.

HÔTEL MEURICE, 228 Rue de Rivoli, 1er. U.S. bookings: Inter•Continental Hotels (Telephone: 800-327-0200)

▼

HÔTEL LOTTI: Across the street from the Meurice, the Lotti shares the same perfect shopping location but is a little less grand. Totally renovated last year by Italian craftsmen (the hotel is a member of the Jolly chain of Italy), the Lotti is the choice of many buyers, art dealers, and smart shoppers. It is not quite as expensive as the Meurice. Expensive.

HÔTEL LOTTI, 7 Rue de Castiglione, 1ᵉʳ. U.S. bookings: Jolly Hotels (Telephone: 800-654-1772)

▼

MAYFAIR HOTEL: The best-kept secret in Paris, the Mayfair is one block from the Meurice and the Lotti. There's no doorman, no hoopla. You could pass by without ever knowing what's within. The Mayfair is small, intimate, and family-run, with a very well-dressed and knowing clientele. The rooms aren't quite as grand as those in the other two hotels but are so beautifully done in the Regency style that you will be quite comfortable. There's even a hair dryer in the bathroom. One block from Concorde, a few steps off the Rue de Rivoli, this hotel might just offer the best deal in Paris in terms of the amount of elegance you get for the amount of money. Moderate.

MAYFAIR HOTEL, 3 Rue Rouget de Lisle, 1ᵉʳ. U.S. bookings: Jacques de Larsay (Telephone: 800-223-1510)

Hotel Hints

The day we met hotel broker Jacques Bacon at his office (Jacques de Larsay, Inc.), we did not fall in love with him. In fact, we weren't even certain we trusted him. He proposed we add to the book a group of small but special hotels in France—not the big touristy hotels but the special little finds that offer charm and, sometimes, a bargain. He gave us a list. We stayed in each to check them out. We now trust M. Bacon so implicitly that we can tell you, if none of the three hotels mentioned above are right for you, call Jacques and tell him your needs and your budget. He does have rooms at $100 a night. Try his recommendations, just as we do. Or book one of the hotels below by calling his toll-free number (800-223-1510).

RELAIS CHRISTINE/PAVILLON DE LA REINE: Twin hotels, one on each side of town. The Relais is a famous hotel created out of a 15th-century abbey right in the heart of Left Bank shopping, near the Seine and the Buci *marché*, offering total charm, wood beam ceilings, and duplex apartments. The Pavillon de la Reine has matching rooms (and duplexes), but it is right on the Place des Vosges, so you are in the trendiest part of town. Total luxury in both places. Expensive.

RELAIS CHRISTINE, 3 Rue Christine, 6^e
PAVILLON DE LA REINE, 28 Place des Vosges, 4^e

▼

FRANÇOIS PREMIER: A beautiful new hotel two blocks from the Champs-Élysées and around the corner from the Hotel George V to give you prime-time, uptown shopping. This hotel is on the François-1er side of the Champs-Élysées, so you can visit all the designer shops on the Rue François-1er and move right to the 16e. A modern hotel done with European flair; the rooms are not overly large but are tastefully designed, and everything is new and fresh—no old-world dusty lampshades. A little more expensive than others of its kind, but there are no surprises here. Moderate to expensive.

FRANÇOIS PREMIER, 7 Rue Magellan, 8^e

HÔTEL BALZAC: An old hotel that was recently modernized to combine a deluxe visit to Paris with an intimate hotel. Some rooms are complete with a stunning view of the Eiffel Tower. Located at the top of the Etoile, right off the Champs-Élysées, on the "other" side from François-1er. The Rue Balzac is a teeny-tiny street; this is a teeny hotel with only seventy charming rooms. A real find. Moderate to expensive.

HÔTEL BALZAC, 6 Rue Balzac, 8^e

▼

QUEEN ELIZABETH: Old-fashioned with the heavy velvet drapes and the beautiful old furniture. The halls are beginning to need work, but you are around the corner from the Hôtel George V and the prices are a tad lower than the other little hotels we've told you about in the area. Moderate.

QUEEN ELIZABETH, 41 Avenue Pierre 1er de Serbie, 8^e

▼

HÔTEL SAINTS-PÈRES: This small hotel has the tiniest rooms in France but a great location on the Left Bank and an excellent price. Fashion buyers stay here, as do fashion editors. The most famous room in the house, #100, has a fresco on the ceiling, and is worth seeing or booking ahead, if you like a rococo giggle. Otherwise the rooms are modern and spare; but the lobby is a breath of spring, with its glass-enclosed patio and small bamboo bar. Moderate.

HÔTEL SAINTS-PÈRES, 65 Rue des Saints-Pères, 6^e

Getting There

While getting to Paris may seem easy enough—after all, most major carriers fly there—we have discovered a few secrets that might make getting there more fun ... and less expensive.

▼ Not only are winter airfares always the best prices, but they are often accompanied by promotional ticketing gimmicks—like: You pay for one ticket and get the second ticket at half price ... no matter what class service you book. This means that, given the right promotional deal, two people can fly to Paris for about $800.

▼ If you care to travel between January and the end of March, try a ticket broker such as Moment's Notice (hot line: 212-750-9111), which is a firm specializing in selling package trips that no one else has bought—at discounted prices. Moment's Notice, which normally requires a membership fee, once was offering real-live Pan American World Airways tickets to anyone—no membership fee—who wanted them within seven days of departure. It was a guaranteed ticket on a guaranteed flight; you just couldn't get it more than seven days prior to departure. The price was about 30% less than the deepest discounted fare offered by the airline at that time.

▼ Packages that include airfare and hotel always give you good prices, especially if you can get those prices guaranteed in dollars, which is possible through many big wholesalers, airlines, and hotels. If the dollar is depressingly low, or merely unstable enough to make you nervous, look carefully at deals in which prices are frozen in U.S. dollars. Car rental agencies also have some of these offerings.

▼ We like the Rail N Drive package that Avis offers (page 202), since it is simply the best deal in France . . . or the United States. Avis has also coordinated this promotion with Air France, so you can get a fly-rail-drive package, in dollars, that is spectacular. Of course, you don't have to fly Air France to get the Rail N Drive part, but you can compare this price with other airlines and see who comes out best.

▼ Air France doesn't advertise this, but if you book a trip to Paris through Jet Vacations (800-JET-0999), you will get a charter price on a regularly scheduled Air France flight! You could call Air France and book the exact same ticket and pay more for it (if you really wanted to do something so stupid). Repeat: Although Jet Vacations offers charter rates, they are not operating no-name charter planes. You will fly on regularly scheduled Air France flights. But there are a limited number of seats, so be advised. In-flight movies and stereo are complimentary, there's duty-free shopping on the plane, and the seats are guaranteed. This may not be the least expensive way to get to Paris, but it is one of the best, and it is far less expensive than regular rates on Air France.

▼ Air France is part owner of an airline called Air Inter, which is your basic domestic carrier throughout France. For those who are not French residents, there is a France Pass. You cannot buy this ticket in France, so stay awake: The ticket costs a flat fee (less than $250), it is valid for one month, and it allows unlimited travel to any of thirty French cities for any seven days during that month.

2 ▾ DETAILS

Shopping Hours

In France, almost all stores are closed on Sunday and Monday. If they open on Monday at all, it is after lunch, about 3 P.M. In Paris, however, *stores are open Monday, or part of Monday.* Always ask the concierge, or call the shop on a Monday if you want verification. Summer hours may differ from winter hours (longer openings in the evening; Saturday closings), and many stores in Paris close for lunch on Saturday during the summer.

Outside of Paris, most stores close every day for two hours for lunch.

The entire month of August may be unusual. Most of France closes down on August 15 for the Feast of the Assumption. Bastille Day, July 14, also is a big closing day—although many Parisian retailers try to take advantage of the crowds in the streets and open shop for extra business. (Likewise, some stores will be open in Paris on August 15, but none will be open in the countryside.) Drugstores and charcuteries are open on big holidays, but big stores certainly are not. While the old-time rumor that Paris is dead in August has been laid to rest, some stores do close for two weeks of vacation in August without even sending a postcard to advise you. We once threw our bags into the lobby of the Meurice and charged down the street at a fast trot to catch the sale at Sonia Rykiel on the Rue du faubourg-Saint-Honoré, only to discover that the shop was closed tight for *vacances.* Yipes!

Most stores in France open at 9:30 to 10

A.M. and remain open until 7 to 7:30 P.M. They may be open more during the Christmas season. Stores usually are open on saints' days but close on national holidays; ask your concierge.

Size Conversion Chart

WOMEN'S DRESSES, COATS, AND SKIRTS

American	3	5	7	9	11	12	13	14	15	16	18
Continental	36	38	38	40	40	42	42	44	44	46	48
British	8	10	11	12	13	14	15	16	17	18	20

WOMEN'S BLOUSES AND SWEATERS

American	10	12	14	16	18	20
Continental	38	40	42	44	46	48
British	32	34	36	38	40	42

WOMEN'S SHOES

American	5	6	7	8	9	10
Continental	36	37	38	39	40	41
British	3½	4½	5½	6½	7½	8½

CHILDREN'S CLOTHING

American	3	4	5	6	6X
Continental	98	104	110	116	122
British	18	20	22	24	26

CHILDREN'S SHOES

American	8	9	10	11	12	13	1	2	3
Continental	24	25	27	28	29	30	32	33	34
British	7	8	9	10	11	12	13	1	2

MEN'S SUITS

American	34	36	38	40	42	44	46	48
Continental	44	46	48	50	52	54	56	58
British	34	36	38	40	42	44	46	48

MEN'S SHIRTS

American	14½	15	15½	16	16½	17	17½	18
Continental	37	38	39	41	42	43	44	45
British	14½	15	15½	16	16½	17	17½	18

MEN'S SHOES

American	7	8	9	10	11	12	13
Continental	39½	41	42	43	44½	46	47
British	6	7	8	9	10	11	12

MEN'S HATS

American	6⅞	7⅛	7¼	7⅜	7½
Continental	55	56	58	59	60
British	6¼	6⅞	7⅛	7¼	7⅜

Getting Around

P aris is laid out in a system of zones called *arrondissements*, which circle around from inside to outside. When France adopted the Zip Code method for its mail, Parisians incorporated the *arrondissement* number into the Zip Code as the last two digits. Thus a Zip Code of 75016 means the address is in the 16th *arrondissement* (16^e). You'll find the *arrondissement* information and this small map valuable in planning your shopping expeditions. Check the map frequently, however, since you may think that 1er and 16e are far apart, when in actuality you can walk the distance and have a great time doing so. (Take the Rue du faubourg-Saint-Honoré toward the Champs-Élysées and you even get the 8e free.)

Note that the abbreviation for *arrondissement* is the letter *e*, not the letter *a*, so if you see a number with a small *e* written after it, this number signifies the *arrondissement*. The first *arrondissement*, however, is written 1er. Know-

PARIS ARRONDISSEMENTS

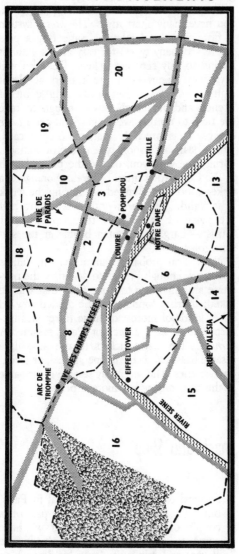

ing the proper *arrondissement* is essential to getting around rapidly in Paris.

To get around on a rapid shopping spree, you have many alternatives. The *métro* system is fast, clean, and relatively safe. Buy a pass (there are many types) for easy access without having to buy separate tickets. This also will save you money—you break even at about eight rides. If you can speak a little bit of French and visit Paris often enough to take the time to do this, we suggest you get a *carte orange*. It is precisely that, an orange card, which bears a passport-type photo of yourself. (Bring one with you, or use the photo booth in the Concorde station.) The *carte orange* is a ticket good for unlimited use during the week it is valid. The *carte orange* is about half the price of the weekly ticket pushed for tourists—bargain shopping begins at the station, folks.

Note: You probably cannot get one unless you speak enough French to negotiate the purchase and answer a few questions that will be asked; touristy tourists will be guided toward other kinds of more expensive ticket arrangements such as a *carnet* or Paris sesame. A *carnet* is ten *métro* tickets to use at will; a sesame pass is available in one-, three-, or seven-day varieties. The seven-day sesame is the same as the *carte orange* but more expensive.

Snack and Shop

I t's hard to get a really bad meal in Paris, but we've had a few, so here we pass on a couple of shopping haunts that we have come to depend on. We don't do the Taillevent or Jamin route (even for dinner), so *pardonnez-nous....* We have been to several McDonald's and we also like to eat at *crêpe* stands. Unfortunately, *crêpe* stands move often, and we're still lamenting the fact that the man with the stand at the corner of the Place de la Madeleine has gone on to greener pastures. Maybe he'll be back this summer.

LA CHOPE DES VOSGES: Right on the Place des Vosges, where you certainly want to spend some of your time, you can have lunch, dinner, or simply tea, which is served from 3 P.M. to 7 P.M. With its old-fashioned front, stone interior, and wood beams, the multilevel space has all the charm you want from a neighborhood like this. Prices are low to moderate; there is a fixed-price, full meal for about $15. Reservations: 42-72-64-04.

LA CHOPE DES VOSGES, 22 Place des Vosges, 3ᵉ (Métro: St. Paul)

▼

CHEZ FRANCIS: This is our favorite bistro in all of Paris. Right in the heart of heavy-duty designer country, at the tip of the Avenue Montaigne, the café attracts a large design and fashion crowd at lunch and dinner. We think Sunday lunch is the best treat, but we've been here on Bastille Day (to see the fireworks directly across the bridge) and on New Year's Eve. The Eiffel Tower is right out the window; the giant dragonfly Art Deco chandeliers are also worth staring at. If you are going on the *bateau-mouche,* stop here for lunch first— you get the boats across the street. Prices are moderate. Reservations: 47-23-39-53.

CHEZ FRANCIS, 7 Place de l'Alma, 16ᵉ (Métro: Alma)

▼

LA COUR SAINT-GERMAIN: There is one location near the Champs-Élysées, and the other is right on Boulevard Saint-Germain, smack dab in the middle of the Left Bank's most popular area. The two restaurants offer identical meals and the same ambience, although the Left Bank one is a bit more touristy and crowded. They both have fabulous meals at a fixed price; the decor is adorable, and you will have a delicious dinner for about $15. You can choose from about eight different menus. Dessert is extra. This is our single best food find in Paris.

LA COUR SAINT-GERMAIN
   156 Boulevard Saint-Germain, 6ᵉ (Reservations: 43-26-85-49) (Métro: Saint-Germain-des-Prés)
   18 Rue Marbeuf, 8ᵉ (Reservations: 47-23-84-25) (Métro: F. D. Roosevelt)

▼

A PRIORI THÉ: Certainly there are fancier places in Paris to have tea (like any of the grand hotels), but there aren't too many places that are more funky—or fun for the shopper. This small tea garden is inside the Galerie Vivienne, one of Paris's most adorable, most authentic, most creative retail spaces. The tea shop is sort of like a French diner, with wicker chairs—it is far from elegant. But there is nothing finer than to sip tea and stare in the window at Casa Lopez and watch the crowd float by.

A PRIORI THÉ, Galerie Vivienne, 6 Rue Vivienne, 2ᵉ (Métro: Bourse)

Shopping Services

S hopping in Paris is either extremely simple because you limit yourself to the very obvious areas, or very complicated because you *know* how much is out there, and that you couldn't possibly conquer it even if all Paris were divided into three parts and you had a month to shop each of them.

Where there's confusion, there's a business. Wives of Americans in business in Paris who cannot get green cards to work in France and are sort of at the mercy of their own imaginations and connections very often set up shopping services. If you use this book properly, you should not need a shopping service. However, you should know that they exist.

Ask your concierge and specify if you want an American or not. Expect to pay an hourly rate with a minimum. Car and driver are extra. Or you can do what our friend Gloria used to do: Ask the hotel to hire a baby-sitter for you for a morning or a day. This usually costs $6 to $8 an hour. Ask for a young, hip, attractive baby-sitter who speaks English. When the baby-sitter comes, ask her to take you shopping.

If you have no time to shop for yourself and want someone to go out and do the buying for you while you spend all your time at the Louvre, there are other buying services that will do this for you.

Shopping Secrets

I f you are looking for some pointers on where to get the best bargains and don't know where to begin, you may want to start at your hotel. If you are a VIP guest at the Inter•Continental hotel, or if you are staying at the Meurice and show your copy of this book, you may get a special *Paris Guide Confidential*, which is a tiny gray and beige booklet filled with ads for shops that tells you what they sell and what kind of gift or discount (either 5% or 10%) they will give you for shopping there. Included in the booklet is an ad for a shoppers' excursion of no more than six people with an English-speaking guide who will take you to the stores. The tours are conducted Tuesday through Saturday from 1 to 5:30 P.M., and cost about $50. You ride in a minibus, are picked up at your hotel, and are taken to all the shops in the hotel booklet. You may reserve this tour even if you are not a hotel guest. Write or call Mary Beth Behrent, Insider's Shopping Tour of Paris, 2 Avenue Vion-Whitcomb, Paris 75016; Telephone: 46-47-81-01.

Figaro, the French publisher, has also gotten into the shopping-services business by offering an annual *Guide Shopping* which is very much like the one that the Meurice and Inter•Continental have, only bigger. There are names and addresses of 350 very tony shops at which you can get a 10% discount if you present the coupon in the book. Contact Le Figaro, 25 Avenue Matignon, 75385 Paris.

American Sale Prices vs. European Prices

A s a rule of thumb, the American sale price on a garment equals a 20% to 25% markdown. The second markdown is 40% to 50% of the originally ticketed price, which puts you basically at the whole-sale price. With European-made merchandise, the first markdown covers shipping and duties and the second markdown brings you to the price on landing in the United States; anything less is below the European retail price but above the European wholesale price. As a result, you can often buy European designer merchandise on sale in the United States for the same—or less—than in a retail store in Europe.

Not every European-made garment is cheaper in Europe than in the United States in the first place, and not every European-designed garment is actually *made* in Europe. Not every European designer retail outlet carries the same merchandise.

One of the best tricks to remember when shopping for European bargains in the United States is that the U.S. boutique owner does not want to pay to ship his end-of-season merchandise back to the country of origin. He will do whatever he has to do to get rid of that merchandise and recover some cash. So you can very often find a final reduction of up to 75%. High-fashion clothes have a very short life span. Usually the shopowner would rather sell the clothes at a fraction of their value than store them or sell them to a jobber. He may give them to charity for a tax deduction, or he may have one hell of a sale. Ask to get on the mailing list; ask for sale dates. Don't be embarrassed to be a "sale only" customer—store managers value these customers and seek their patronage when they have merchandise to move out. Some particular points to remember:

▾ More and more franchises are moving toward international pricing, so the same merchandise costs the same price everywhere.

▾ A European sale price on European designer merchandise is probably less than in the United States, but if the dollar is weak, do not assume automatic savings.

▾ Shop franchised designer shops for the largest selection or for crazy sales; otherwise, the best deals are in other areas.

Shipping from Paris

Shipping anything from Paris begins before you get there. If you are smart, or serious, you will do some homework before you leave and have your shipping arrangements partly made before you even arrive.

Contact a shipper in your hometown, or in New York, and work together to make sure all your shopping days are pleasant. The shipper should be able to act as your agent; the buying game will be much less tense once you have someone to take care of you.

▾ When you arrive in Paris, plan to meet with your chosen shipping agent. Make the appointment from the United States, and meet the agent as soon as possible so you can feel confident and on top of things.

▾ Explain to your agent the kinds of things you are planning to buy and the approximate number of pieces. The answer is not a pair of brown shoes and a handbag to match. Tell him if it's valuable antiques, merely used furniture, original Picasso canvases, or what. Discuss a cost estimate and make sure you have a complete understanding of how the system works and how much you are paying per cubic meter. (About $200 is the right price, by the way.) Ask about groupage in a container or if you should have your own container.

▼ If you can't fill a container, ask how long you will have to wait for space in a container. This could be a long wait.

▼ Discuss the connections to be made from New York to your hometown. Ask if the package is indeed shipped through New York, or another port city that may be closer to you. New York gets more packages, and routing probably will save you time. The proper shipper should be able to arrange direct shipping.

▼ Find out if you need a customhouse broker to meet your goods and clear them, or if the shipping agent does this. Is this part of the shipping cost, or is there an additional fee?

▼ Your shipping agent will give you a book of receipts in duplicate. When you purchase your pieces, you have the antiques dealer fill out the receipt with a complete description of what you bought and the price. You keep one receipt on your pad; the dealer keeps the other. You do not pay the dealer. After you have made all your purchases, you return to your shipping agent with your book of receipts. He totals the bill and you pay him directly—for the purchases and the shipping all at once. Then the shipper gets your goods from the various dealers, and he pays them. He crates and packs your items and puts them on the plane or ship you have agreed on. *Bon voyage.*

▼ Take two Polaroid pictures of everything you buy—one for your records and one for the shipper. It's very hard to prove damages on an antique piece without a picture. It's also good to have a picture of what you bought, because human memory is so frail that you will imagine you bought something very different after you haven't seen it for three days.

▼ All items a hundred years old or older have to be approved for export by the Commission of the Louvre. Your shipper should handle this for you. If you go to the Louvre, you want to see Mona Lisa or maybe even I. M. Pei, but you do not want to see the commissioner. However, make sure you are in town until the approvals are won, lest there be any snafus.

▼ If the item is less than a hundred years old, you do not have to go to the commissioner. But you do have to pay to U.S. Customs.

▼ Shippers who have been recommended to us by various dealers on a consistent basis over a period of years include:

Nlle Atlantic
62 Rue Mirabeau
Ivry-sur-Seine, France

Camard
28 Rue Christino Garcia
La Plaine Saint-Denis, France

Art Transit
10 Rue Leibnitz
Paris 71018, France

U.S. Customs and Duties

To make your reentry into the United States as smooth as possible, follow these tips:

▼ Know the rules and stick to them!
▼ Don't try to smuggle anything.

▼ Be polite and cooperative (up until the point when they ask you to strip, anyway . . .).

Remember:

▼ You are currently allowed to bring in $400 worth of merchandise per person, duty-free. Before you leave the United States, verify this amount with one of the U.S. Customs offices. This amount does change, and if you miss the news item in the paper, you may be cheating yourself out of a good deal. Each member of the family is entitled to the deduction; this includes infants.

▼ You pay a flat 10% duty on the next $1,000 worth of merchandise. This is extremely simple and is worth doing. We're talking about the very small sum of $100 to make life easy—and crime-free.

▼ Duties thereafter are based on a product-type basis. They vary tremendously per item.

▼ The head of the family can make a joint declaration for all family members. The "head of the family" need not be male. Whoever is the head of the family, however, should take the responsibility for answering any questions the Customs officers may ask. Answer questions honestly, firmly, and politely. Have receipts ready, and make sure they match the information on the landing card. Don't be forced into a story that won't wash under questioning. If you tell a little lie, you'll be labeled as a fibber and they'll tear your luggage apart.

▼ You count into your $400 per person everything you obtain while abroad—this includes toothpaste (if you bring the unfinished tube back with you), gifts, items bought in duty-free shops, gifts for others, the items that other people asked you to bring home for them, and—get this—even alterations.

▼ Have the Customs registration slips for your personally owned goods in your wallet or easily available. If you wear a Cartier watch, for example, whether it was bought in the United States or in Europe ten years ago, should you be questioned about it, produce the registration slip. If you cannot prove that you took a foreign-made item out of the United States with you, you may be forced to pay duty on it!

▼ The unsolicited gifts you mailed from abroad do not count in the $400-per-person rate. If the value of the gift is more than $50, you pay duty when the package comes into the country. Remember, it's only one unsolicited gift per person, and you cannot mail them to yourself.

▼ Do not attempt to bring in any illegal food items—dairy products, meats, fruits, or vegetables (coffee is OK). Generally speaking, if it's alive, it's *verboten*.

▼ We don't need to tell you it's tacky to bring in drugs and narcotics.

▼ Antiques must be a hundred years old to be duty-free. Provenance papers will help (so will permission actually to export the antiquity, since it could be an item of national cultural significance).

▼ Dress for success. People who look like "hippies" get stopped at Customs more than average folks. Women who look like a million dollars, who are dragging their fur coats, have first-class baggage tags on their luggage, and carry Gucci handbags, but declare they have bought nothing, are equally suspicious.

▼ Any bona fide work of art is duty-free whether it was painted fifty years ago or just yesterday; the artist need not be famous.

3 ▼ MONEY MATTERS

Paying Up

Whether you use cash, traveler's check, or credit card, you probably are paying for your purchase in a currency different from American dollars.

For the most part, we recommend using a credit card—especially in fancy stores. Plastic is the safest to use, provides you with a record of your purchases (for U.S. Customs as well as your books), and makes returns a lot easier. Credit-card companies, because they often are associated with banks, may give the best exchange rates. We even know of people who have "made money" by charging on a credit card. That's because the price you pay as posted in dollars is translated on the day your credit slip clears the credit-card company (or bank) office, not the day of your purchase. Say the franc is trading at 5.8. Your hotel may give you only 5.5 francs per dollar when you convert your money. American Express probably will give you a higher rate of exchange, maybe even as high as 5.75. You gain.

The bad news about credit cards is that you can overspend easily, and you may come home to a stack of bills. If currency is fluctuating wildly and the dollar happens to fall, you also end up paying more for your purchases than you planned. The day you walk into Bernard Perris and blow your wad on a suit, you walk out thinking you have paid $600 for the suit. Three days later, the paperwork is done on your charge slip and the dollar has fallen— you may end up paying $650 for the suit.

On the other hand, one extra benefit about a credit card is that you often get delayed billing, so that you may have a month or two to raise some petty cash.

If you go to a shop that does not honor any of the cards you hold but does have a display of cards in the window, ask them to pull out their credit forms to find the names (and pictures) of their reciprocal bank cards. Chances are you can make a match. Access, a common European credit card, happens to be the same as MasterCard—yet this is rarely advertised.

If you happen to be given a book of discount coupons by your hotel or tour guide, you will also notice that you get a 10% discount for cash but only a 5% discount when you use credit cards. Storekeepers much prefer you to pay in cash. Remember this also when you are bargaining at the market of Saint-Ouen. A credit-card transaction costs the retailer 2% to 5%. If you pay cash, you should be able to get that discount.

Traveler's checks are a must—for safety's sake. Shop around a bit, compare the various companies that issue checks, and make sure your checks are insured against theft or loss. While we like and use American Express traveler's checks, they are not the only safe game in town.

BankAmerica provides traveler's checks in various currencies, and for $5 more gives you an insurance package that is wonderful. Thomas Cook provides traveler's checks free and in foreign currencies. American Express can provide traveler's checks in francs. This is a big plus when changing checks at hotels or shops, because you will have a guaranteed rate of exchange. *However*, you must buy the checks through a bank and at their rate of exchange. You may make or lose on this deal.

Currency Exchange

A s we've already mentioned, currency exchange rates vary tremendously. The rate announced in the paper (it's in the *Herald Tribune* every day) is the official bank exchange rate and does not particularly apply to tourists. Even by trading your money at a bank you will not get the same rate of exchange that's announced in the papers.

▼ You will get a better rate of exchange for a traveler's check than for cash because there is less paperwork involved for banks, hotels, etc. Per hundred dollars, expect to save $5 for using traveler's checks.

▼ The rate of exchange you get is usually not negotiable with that establishment. While you can shop for the best rate available, you cannot haggle for a better rate from a certain source.

▼ Hotels generally give the least favorable rate of exchange. Shops may negotiate on the rate of exchange. Say the item you buy costs the equivalent of $40 and you sign over a $50 traveler's check. The shopkeeper may ask you the rate of exchange, or say something like, "Let's see—today the dollar is trading at ..." He (or you) then will pull out a calculator and figure out how much change you will get. If you have bought a lot, you may ask for a more favorable rate of exchange on your change, or bargain a bit. Exclusive shops will be insulted at this maneuver (use credit cards there, anyway). Likewise, the time involved in getting a better rate may be so preposterous that it doesn't matter how expensive your hotel is. One day we decided to go to one of the change bureaus at Opéra that was giving a higher rate than our hotel. After one half hour in line, we quit. It would have taken three hours to reach the head of that line. We would have saved $3.

▼ Do not expect a bank to give you a better rate than your hotel, if a commission is charged. We've generally found the best rate of exchange at the American Express office. They do not charge a commission. If you use a bank, do not continue to change small sums of money, as commissions can add up.

▼ If you want to change money back to dollars when you leave a country, remember that you will pay a higher rate for them. You are now "buying" dollars rather than "selling" them. Therefore, never change more money than you think you will need, unless you stockpile for another trip.

▼ Have some foreign currency on hand for arrivals. After a lengthy transatlantic flight, you will not want to stand in line at some airport booth to get your cab fare. You'll pay a very high rate of exchange and be wasting your precious bathtub time. Your home bank or local currency exchange office can sell you small amounts of foreign currency. No matter how much of a premium you pay for this money, the convenience will be worth it. We ask for $50 worth of currency for each country we are visiting. This will pay for the taxi to the hotel, tips, and the immediate necessities until you decide where to change the rest of your money.

▼ Keep track of what you pay for your currency. If you are going to several countries, or you must make several money-changing trips to the cashier, write down the sums. When you get home and wonder what you did with all the money you used to have, it'll be easier to trace your cash. When you are budgeting, adjust to the rate you paid for the money, not the rate you read in the newspaper.

▼ Make mental comparative rates for quick price reactions. Know the conversion rate for

$50 and $100 so that within an instant you can make a judgment. If you're still interested in an item, slow down and figure out the accurate price.

How to Get Cash Overseas

We've run out of cash on more international trips than we like to admit.

If you do run out of money, know where to turn so you can do so during business hours. Holidays, saints' days, weekends, and late nights are not good times to be without funds. If you think you can sail into your deluxe hotel and present your credit card at the cashier for an instant injection of cash or the redemption of a personal check from your U.S. bank, think again.

Go to American Express for quick cash. Card members may draw on their cards for cash advances or may cash personal checks. (*Never travel without your checkbook.*)

It's all a relatively simple transaction—you write a personal check at a special desk and show your card; it is approved; you go to another desk and get the money in the currency you request. Allow about a half hour for the whole process, unless there are long lines. Usually you get the credit advance on your card at the same desk.

Bank Machines

Bank cash machines are being used in Europe, but don't count on finding them everywhere you go, and don't be surprised if they won't take your card. We tried several machines in France and found them fun—like slot machines in Vegas. We were never certain if we'd get our card back, and we never got any money from one. Our favorite was the one with these little words in lights:

"Please introduce your card."

This is all in French, mind you. We insert card.

"Your card is not remembered."

Reject.

However, American Express machines will dispense cash if you are already set up for this service. Other bank cards are now forming international networks to allow you to use your card in some foreign locations. Ask for addresses before you leave home.

Send Money

You can have money sent to you from home, a process that usually takes about two days. Money can be wired through Western Union (someone brings them the cash or a certified check, and WU does the rest—this may take up to a week) or through an international money order, which is cleared by telex through the bank where you cash it. Money can be wired from bank to bank, but this works simply only with major banks from big cities and that have European branches or sister banks. Banks usually charge a nice fat fee for doing you this favor. If you have a letter of credit, however, and a corresponding bank that is expecting you, you will have little difficulty getting your hands on some extra green . . . or pink or blue or orange.

In an emergency, the American consulate may lend you money. You must repay this money. (There's no such thing as a free lunch.)

Détaxe

T he *détaxe* is a 12% to 33% tax that is levied on all goods, just like a sales tax in the United States. The French pay it automatically. Tourists can get a refund on it. The amount of the tax credit varies with the type of item bought. The furniture tax is 18%; perfume is 33%.

The basic *détaxe* system works pretty much like this:

▼ You are shopping in a store with prices marked on the merchandise. This is the true price of the item that any tourist or any national must pay. (We're assuming you are in a department store with fixed prices, not a flea market.) If you are a national, you pay the price without thinking twice. If you are a tourist who plans to leave the country within six months, you ask a salesperson, "What is the minimum expenditure in this store for the export refund?" The rate varies from shop to shop, although the minimum is set by law. Currently the *détaxe* is refunded to a person who spends 1,200 francs or more. However, some of the really fancy, big-name, big-deal stores ask you to spend 1,500 francs for the *détaxe* (at Louis Vuitton, it is 1,800 francs!). Always ask before you assume.

▼ All stores have a minimum purchase requirement before they will grant you the discount. Let's say you buy piecemeal—you get a $40 sweater one day and return to the store a week later and buy, say, a $10 mascara, two $6 pairs of pantyhose, and some underwear for $22. Then you dash back in a day later for a birthday present for your sister—a silk blouse for $60 and one just like it for yourself, another $60. You will have paid a total of $204 for the three-day shopping excursion. Had you done some heavy-duty shopping and done it all at once, you could have gotten the discount, which means all these purchases would have cost you about $175!

▼ Once you know the minimum, judge accordingly if you will make a smaller purchase or come back another time for a big haul. Only you know how much time your schedule will permit for shopping. Remember that on a $10 purchase, the 20% saving is too minimal to make *détaxe* meaningful. Keep the discount in perspective.

▼ If you are going to another European country, consider the VAT or *détaxe* policy there. For example, you probably won't get the *détaxe* in Italy. You'll get the VAT in England, but it's a set 15%, not variable, as in France.

▼ If you go for the *détaxe,* budget your time to allow for the paperwork. It takes about fifteen minutes to fill out the forms, and may take twenty to sixty minutes for you to be processed if you are shopping in a big department store during the tourist season. We've done the paperwork in less than five minutes, so don't be frightened. But do allow more time than you need, just in case.

You will need your passport number (but not necessarily the passport itself) for the forms. The space that asks for your address is asking for your hotel. The name of the hotel will suffice, not its entire address. (Don't be so surprised; few people know the street address of a hotel!)

▼ After the papers are filled in, they will be given to you with an envelope. Sometimes the envelope has a stamp on it; sometimes it is blank (you must provide the postage stamp before you leave the country); sometimes it has a special government frank that serves as a stamp. If you don't understand what's on your envelope, ask.

▼ When you are leaving the country, go to the Customs official who serves the *détaxe* papers. DO THIS BEFORE YOU CLEAR REGULAR CUSTOMS OR SEND OFF YOUR LUGGAGE. The Customs officer has the right to ask you to show him (or her) the merchandise you bought and are taking out of the country. Whether the officer sees your purchases or not, he or she will stamp the papers, keeping a set (which will be processed) and giving you another set, in the envelope. You then mail the envelope (usually it is preprinted with the shop's name and address or will have been addressed by the shop for you). The Customs officer keeps the specially franked envelopes, sometimes. Don't worry, they'll be mailed.

▼ When the papers get back to the shop and the government has notified the shop that their set of papers has been registered, the store will then grant you the discount through a refund. This can be done on your credit card, of which they will have made a dual pressing, or through a personal check, which will come to you in the mail, usually three months later. (It will be in a foreign currency—your bank may charge you to change it into dollars.)

Okay, that's how the system works. Now here are the fine points:

The way in which you get your discount is somewhat negotiable!

At the time of the purchase, discuss your options for the refund with the retailer. Depending on how much you have bought, how big a store it is, or how cute you are, you may get a more favorable situation. There are three different ways in which you can get the refund; in order of preference to the tourist they are:

1. The retailer sells you the merchandise at the cheapest price possible, including the dis-

count, and therefore actually takes a loss on income until the government reimburses him. For example: The bottle of fragrance you want costs $50. The discount is $7.50. The best possible deal you could ever get is for the retailer to charge you $42.50 flat, give you the *détaxe* papers, and explain to you that he will not get the rest of his money unless you process the papers properly. Being as honorable as you are, of course you process the papers. We've been offered this method at Catherine and at Bottega Veneta.

2. Almost as simple is the credit-card refund. You pay for the purchase, at the regular retail price, with a major credit card. Then your plate is restamped for a refund slip, marked for the amount of the *détaxe*. You sign both slips at the time of the purchase. When the papers come back to the retailer, the shop puts through the credit slip. The credit may appear on the same monthly statement as the original bill or on a subsequent bill. Just remember to check for the credits.

3. You pay the regular retail price, with cash, traveler's check, or credit card. This is the most widely used method. You are given the forms, you go through the refund process, you get on your plane and go home. Several months later (usually about three) you get a check in the mail made out for the refund. This check is in the currency of the country in which you made the purchase and will have to be converted to dollars and cents, a process for which your bank may charge you a percentage or a fee. Or you can go to Deak Perera or another currency broker and get the money in the currency of origin to save for your next trip to that country. Either way, it's a pain in the neck.

Returns and Refunds

American outlets should repair European-bought merchandise, provided it's genuine. There may or may not be a fee for this; the matter may be negotiable.

If your credit-card bill shows a purchase that you have no recollection of making, or if the signatures on the credit-card slips don't match yours or your husband's, notify the credit-card company or bank immediately. Do not pay that portion of the bill until you get further clarification. Bank cards usually just list your charges rather than provide a copy of the sales slip. You may not even recognize the names of some of the shops you have been in. We know one woman who had a $200 charge on her bank card from Orly in Paris. Since she did not fly in or out of Orly International Airport, she was certain it was a mistake, and so notified the credit-card company. She did not pay that part of her bill. The bank provided her with a copy of the sales slip; she verified her own signature and had to admit that Orly must be the name of a shop she could not even remember visiting. (It happens to be a discount scarf shop on the Rue de Rivoli in Paris.)

It always will be difficult to handle foreign financial matters through the mails. Use credit cards whenever possible, since they will expedite matters somewhat; have your sales slips and charge records and a copy of your side of the correspondence with the vendor and the bank or credit-card company; persevere, but have patience. The better the reputation of the shop or designer you buy from, the better your chances of not being ripped off in the first place and of making returns for refund. Some bank cards may set a limit on international returns or refunds. Ask before you leave home.

One Last Calculating Thought

U nless you have a Ph.D. in mathematics from MIT, we suggest you keep a calculator in your purse at all times. Furthermore, it should be the kind that uses batteries. Solar-run calculators are very cute, but your purse is dark inside, and many shops are, too. There's nothing worse than trying to do a hard bit of negotiating when your calculator won't calculate. If you use your calculator frequently, or if your children like to play with it as a toy, buy new batteries before you leave on the trip.

4 ▼ THE BUSINESS OF BARGAINS

To Market, to Market

One of the difficulties in shopping in Paris is deciding which markets to visit and which to pass up. Unlike most other cities that usually have one or two good markets, Paris is crawling with them. There are actually dozens of them, and it's impossible to get to them all unless you spend a month doing little else.

Remember:

▼ Dress simply; the richer you look, the higher the price. If you wear an engagement ring, or have one of those wedding bands that spells RICH AMERICAN in *pavé* diamonds, leave it in the hotel safe. We like to wear blue jeans and to try to fit in as best we can.

▼ Check with your hotel concierge about the neighborhood where the market is located. It may not be considered safe for a woman to go there alone, or after dark. We don't want to be chauvinistic or paranoid, but crime in market areas can be higher than in tourist areas—especially outdoor markets.

▼ Have a lot of change with you. It's difficult to bargain and then offer a large bill and ask for change. As a bargaining point, be able to say you only have so much cash on hand.

▼ If you look like a tourist, the price may start out higher; if you don't know much about what you are buying, the price also may start higher. You do not need to speak any specific language, however, to make a good deal. Bargaining is an international language of emotion, hand signs, facial expressions, etc. If you feel you are being taken, walk away.

▼ Branded merchandise sold on the street can be hot or counterfeit.

▼ Go early if you expect the best selection. Go late if you want to make the best deals.

▼ Never trust anyone (except a qualified shipping agent) to mail anything for you.

▼ Make sure you are buying something you can legally bring back to the States; don't buy tortoiseshell boxes or combs, because those beauties will be impounded by U.S. Customs.

▼ Don't pay the asking price on *brocante* (used junk) unless you want to give the vendor the privilege of telling all his friends what a chump you are.

In Paris, many market areas are so famous that they have no specific street address. Usually it's enough to name the market to a cabbie, but ask your concierge if you need more in the way of directions. Buses usually service market areas; the *métro* goes everywhere and usually is the best bet.

Big Flea Markets of Paris

M any people ask us what they can do on a Sunday when all the stores are closed. Why, go to a flea market, of course! All the stores are not closed on Sunday, by the by—but most of them are. (The Beaubourg is amazingly populated on Sunday and the stalls along the river are also open.)

There is no question in our minds that the single best place to go is the flea market at Saint-Ouen, which most people just call the

Flea Market (Marché aux Puces). It may be the world's largest (over three thousand dealers) and even puts the Rose Bowl (in Pasadena, California) in the shade. Our hearts beat faster and we feel a little like drug addicts getting ready for a fix when we even think about the wonders of this market. All other markets pale in comparison, but other markets are easier to shop and closer to your hotel. Saint-Ouen should be done as an all-day adventure. Don't go if you have only two hours. The market offers mostly furniture and decorative items; there are three thousand vendors, so you can bet there's a good bit of everything. Vendors selling new merchandise line the street on the walk from the *métro* (Porte de Clignancourt) in what is called the Marché Malik. The actual market you seek is about a mile away. The market is open Saturday, Sunday, and Monday.

The Marché aux Puces was very different in reality than our fantasy of it, so you, too, may be surprised. It takes about an hour to get from central Paris to Porte de Clignancourt on the *métro*; then you step out and see vendor after vendor in rows of stalls selling mostly brand-new blue jeans. We considered bursting into tears. The famous flea market just sells jeans? Junky handbags? After spending hours working this area looking for something wonderful, we discovered we were in the wrong place! These vendors set up shop to tease the crowds. The real market is about a mile away. There're actually seventy-five acres of flea-market territory out there, and several different buildings, which house stall after stall. Besides the buildings, there are many freestanding stalls and zillions of blankets-on-the-pavement vendors, as well as street hawkers who will push a Cartier watch into your face, swear that it's real, and ask you to make an offer. This isn't anything near the human zoo that Hong Kong is, but it's a far cry from the civilized boulevards you left in central Paris. In fact, it's in a rather dumpy neighborhood that may give you the creeps. It will definitely exhaust you. Wear comfortable shoes, appropriate clothes (don't look too rich), and sunscreen if it's a sunny day. If you are bringing kids with you, bring your stroller. There are several street hawkers who sell toys in this part of the market area.

You will rub shoulders with every nationality, every age, and every bargain hunter in Paris at Clignancourt. If you are claustrophobic, this may not be for you. (Also, as in all flea markets, beware of pickpockets.) The blue-jeans dealers are so thickly distributed that it is hard to get to the good part of the market, and you may find your energy already expended by the time you get to the huts of treasures. There are a few cafés and dives interspersed among the market buildings, so you can get coffee, or steak with french fries, and feel like you've had a wild adventure.

Many of the merchants are in partnership, usually by building or by alley. The Marché Brion, on the corner of Rue des Rosiers and Avenue Michelet, is the priciest and toniest of all the markets, and its stall owners are in partnership. There are now about 250 stands in this part of the market alone. If you are a serious buyer, head here first for the good stuff. (Métro: Porte de Clignancourt)

▼

RUE DE BUCI: The Rue de Buci is behind the church of Saint-Germain-des-Prés. This is a flower and food market that is colorful and quaint and warm and wonderful and worthy of a postcard. Although this is a big antique shop neighborhood, the market does not sell *brocante*. (Métro: Saint-Germain-des-Prés)

▼

PLACE D'ALIGRE: The Place d'Aligre has a covered indoor market (for butcher, etc.), an open flower and vegetable market, several tables devoted to *brocante* dealers, and even a few shops along the way. Betty, a good discount source, is right here, and there's a Felix Potin store that sells groceries and dry goods. The *brocante* is very much of tag-sale quality, and you may be annoyed that you came so far if you were searching for the jewel of the Nile. This market is open every day except Monday but closes at about 1 P.M. While ready-to-wear is sold here, it is exactly what Grandma Jessie would call *dreck*, if you'll pardon her French. The yard goods are good buys from nearby factories. (Métro: Ledru-Rollin or Gare de Lyon)

▼

PUCES DE VANVES: This market is not like any other market; it's more like a bunch of neighbors who all went in together for one of those big five-family garage sales. The market is L-shaped: On the main part of the street are the licensed vendors who pay taxes to the city; on the branch part are the illegal, tag-sale vendors—who are the most fun. The tag-sale people's goods are genuinely of less quality than those of the pros, but together they make for a wonderful hour or two of browsing. If you don't have much time or can't stand the strain of Saint-Ouen, this is a neighborhood affair that is perfect for a Sunday—although it is also open on Saturday. Early birds get the worms, of course. The main part of the market is on the Avenue Georges-Lafenestre. With the legal and the illegal guys, there are almost two hundred vendors here. On the way back to the *métro*, walk through the Sunday fruit and vegetable market one block over on the Boulevard Brune. (Métro: Porte de Vanves)

▼

PUCES DE MONTREUIL: Real people of the world, unite, sing "La Marseillaise," and run out to the *marché* of Montreuil. An immense market that has absorbed three other nearby markets and that has a huge path of illegals that stretches from the *métro* all the way across a bridge to the beginning of the market proper, this is a junk fair with a few diamonds so artfully hidden that just when you are about to throw up your hands in disgust, you strike pay dirt. There's a good selection of *fripes* (used clothes), Victorian bed linens, old hats, new perfumes (look, Mom, who needs *détaxe?*), work clothes, cheap clothes, records, dishes, junk, junk, and more junk. Dealers work this market very thoroughly—it runs a good 10% to 20% cheaper than Saint-Ouen. But it is 50% harder to find anything good. This is for those with a strong heart and a good eye.

You'll exit the *métro* to find yourself in a little neighborhood trading area. Very nice—there are several pleasant bakeries and *crêperies* here. Follow the trail of vendors over the bridge. The market starts once you've crossed the bridge over the highway, in what appears to be a small area, but stretches back for days. There are said to be over a thousand vendors at the *marché* and another thousand illegal vendors lining the path from *métro* to *marché*. (Métro: Porte de Montreuil)

Street Merchants

P aris street merchants come in two categories: imitation and real. Most of the merchants around the department stores— the ones with the carts who seem to be selling such great bargains—work for the department stores. They are fake street merchants.

The guys in front of Saint-Germain-des-Prés are more authentic street merchants—although many of the same guys have been there selling the same stuff for years. But still, it has its charm.

While we cannot complain about these real street merchants in Saint-Germain, we would love to squawk about many of the other real street merchants in Paris. They are so boring! They sell either little birds with plastic wings that whirl around your head or cheap brass bangle bracelets that smell bad. Give us some Dior, boys.

Used Merchandise

The French pride themselves on being a practical people. They rarely throw anything away, they buy only the best quality and use it forever, they hate waste of any sort. But if someone in the family dies, or if someone should fall on hard times, he can sell his fine possessions at a *dépôt-vente*. Or, knowing that good merchandise is being sold, he will frequent a *dépôt-vente*. No one in Paris is ever ashamed to be buying used items. They think it's smart.

We do, too. See our section on page 122 for the names of some famous *dépôt-ventes*.

Tag Sales

The French do not know from tag sales. But they do have weekly neighborhood markets that have a *brocante* day. *Brocante* is used junk that never would really be called antique. It is the same kind of item you see at a tag sale. If this sort of thing interests you, find the market day and take a look.

There are more *brocante* dealers at the big

markets. Big flea markets are licensed by the city of Paris. Each stall owner pays taxes to the city for his stall and the right to be there. But on the fringes of each market are the illegal guys. They traditionally are not dealers but people with leftovers who are selling exactly what you would see at a tag sale.

Antique Clothes

Antique clothes or used clothes are called *fripes* in French and are a big item. You can buy them at markets or from dealers. Almost every *marché* has a few *brocante* dealers who sell old pillowcases and camisoles. If you want a better selection, remember that the Marché Malik at Saint-Ouen is famous for its *fripes*.

Rentals

About Madame's ball gown. The proper place to rent a couture gown is Sommier, 3 Passage Brady, 10ᵉ. The French, being a very practical people, believe in the rental business; therefore, it works. Since Frenchwomen want only the finest quality and are too practical to buy a couture gown for a once-in-a-lifetime formal event, they rent. If it's been your dream to wear a couture gown, you can have a very good choice for about $100 for the night.

French Factory Outlets

Yes, the French have factory outlets right there in Paris. But no, they probably aren't worth your time, energy, or money. Resale shops are fabulous in Paris; if you want a good break on good merchandise, use them. Factory outlets are for French locals. If you're living in France, or have a car and are merely curious, give them a whirl.

Paris Nord

This is the kind of place that sounds great if a French person tells you about it or you happen to read a write-up in a book or magazine. It sounds like everything you know and love—seventy-two shops selling at factory prices, designer goods, overruns, etc. We find you really have to get lucky to make it worthwhile.

The name of the village is the Commercial Center de Paris Nord/Ursine Center. It's about a half-hour drive from Paris, is close to Charles de Gaulle International Airport, and is open from 10 A.M. to 8 P.M. Wednesday through Sunday.

This is a very suburban center. To a tourist, it's in the middle of nowhere. (It is in the middle of nowhere.)

While there certainly are a ton of stores here, and they are in the factory-outlet tradition, most of the names and labels mean little to us. They are low-end or moderately priced goods, pretty much. Designer things are the exception, not the rule.

The prices, as at all factory outlets, may not be so cheap. The merchandise also may be out of style or very old.

Commercial Center-X%

X% is the name of the center, honest. It's at
Île St. Denis and is open Wednesday through
Sunday from 10 A.M. to 8 P.M.

This is not a great neighborhood.

The designers are not big-name, but the
quality is better than it is at Paris Nord.

5 ▼ NEIGHBORHOODS

The *Arrondissements*

The First (1er)

The 1er is one of the smallest *arrondissements*, but it is not the oldest one. (Paris actually began on the Île de la Cité, which is in the 4e. The 1er is a primary shopping area, with several high-rent neighborhoods and four main districts: Louvre, Halles, Palais-Royal, and Vendôme (Tuileries).

The amazing thing about the 1er is the diversity of shopping. You get the wild and crazy, just up from nothing, and still-tarnished feel of Les Halles, with its punk shops, souvenir shops, and crazy boutiques (Mechanic Hair); you get the Rue de Rivoli mobs that fill the department store BHV; and then you get the tourists who pour out of the Louvre near Palais-Royal and fan down the Rue de Rivoli toward Concorde, where they can shop in all the tacky tourist traps until they reach the Rue du faubourg-Saint-Honoré, one of the fanciest streets in Paris.

We always stay at the Meurice, which is in the 1er, so we know this neighborhood really well, and we marvel at the Rue de Rivoli on one side—so incredibly touristy—and the Marché Saint-Honoré, just on the other side of a small block, which is exactly what you came to Paris to see but which no one ever told you was there.

The Second (2e)

The 2e is called Bourse, and consists of four districts: Gaillon, Vivienne, Mail, and Bonne-Nouvelle.

You may not find yourself here too much unless you have the heart of a garmento—as we do—and want to visit the Sentier, which is the garment center. The Galerie Vivienne also is in the 2^e. Essentially the 2^e is behind the 1er and is very businessy and wholesaley—not that charming a place (with exceptions, of course). *Note*: Victoires is on the border of the 1er and 2^e, and it is one of the highlights of Paris.

The Third (3^e)

Nicknamed either Temple or Marais, the 3^e has become popular with the renaissance of the Marais itself and the Place des Vosges (which happens to be on the border of the 3^e and 4^e)—and is a must-do, must-drool on your tour of Paris.

The opening of the Picasso Museum, which is in the 3^e but near the 4^e, and the rebirth of the Place des Vosges (4^e) brought in many tourists, and cute shops have blossomed like rosebuds. There's also a big covered market called the Carreau du Temple, where you can find old clothes (*fripes*) and some nice hand-crafted items. It's open every day except Monday; no designer clothes here. Don't get mixed up between Rue du Temple and Boulevard du Temple.

Boulevard du Temple and that part of the neighborhood backs up to République, and this is a very middle-class, working-class kind of neighborhood that has a good number of discounters and rather shabby outlets that probably aren't worth investigating—and certainly aren't worth your time if you are a Faubourg Saint-Honoré kind of customer.

The Fourth (4e)

This neighborhood backs up on the Marais and the Place des Vosges—which is a very grand and wonderful place to live. At one end it includes the emerging Bastille area; the other actually borders with the 3ᵉ at the Place des Vosges. Not far away there is a famous and very colorful old Jewish neighborhood. The shopping might not be grand in the 4ᵉ, but living on the Île Saint-Louis is far from shabby. And the local church is the Cathedral of Notre-Dame.

The Fifth (5ᵉ)

This is the famous Latin Quarter, or student quarter, which is also called Panthéon. *C'est la Bohème*—it's filled with little cafés and restaurants; it's paradise for book-hunters. There are shops selling *fripes* and jeans, as that seems to be all that people around here wear. There's a large American population in this quarter, and a large Muslim population near the mosque. Open markets are at Carmes, Place Maubert, on Tuesday, Thursday, and Saturday, as well as at Port-Royal on the same days. The Sunday market is at Place Monge.

The Sixth (6ᵉ)

One of the most fun *arrondissements* for tourists and shoppers, the 6ᵉ is called Luxembourg because of the gardens by the same name, or Saint-Germain-des-Prés because of the church and main drag of the same name, which we just shorten to Saint-Germain. The street market on the Rue du Buci, with the fruits, vegetables, and flowers piled high, is a sight for a photographer. The antiques business is clustered here, as is the boutique business. The covered market is on Rue Félibien; there is another street market on Tuesday and Friday at Rue du Cherche-Midi.

The Seventh (7ᵉ)

An expensive area for shopping, it's known as Palais-Bourbon, and districts include: Saint-Thomas-d'Aquin, Invalides, École Militaire, and Gros-Caillou.

There is an open market on Thursday and Saturday in Breteuil at the Avenue de Saxe, a covered market in Gros-Caillou on the Rue Jean Nicot. The Rue Cler reigns as the street for food, serious food. The main shopping streets are Rue de Grenelle (which is also partially in the 6ᵉ) and Rue Saint-Dominique. There are many small shops for rich ladies who just can't go so far as the crass Faubourg Saint-Honoré or the crasser Champs-Élysées. And yes, the Tour Eiffel is in the 7ᵉ.

The Eighth (8ᵉ)

Élysées is the 8ᵉ, which stretches right across some of the best shopping in the world and is nestled between the 1ᵉʳ and the 16ᵉ. One of our favorite shopping jaunts is to walk across these three *arrondissements* in a more or less straight line from the Hôtel Meurice along the Rue du faubourg-Saint-Honoré to Place de l'Alma at the end of Avenue Montaigne. Districts in the 8ᵉ are: Élysées, Madeleine, Europe, and Miromesnil.

The Ninth (9ᵉ)

The 9ᵉ is famous to most of the world as Opéra. This is where Galeries Lafayette, Monoprix, and Au Printemps, as well as Prisunic and every street vendor in Paris are gathered in the most heavy-duty shopping per meter anyplace in the world. American Express also is in this neighborhood, if you need more money. And frankly, who doesn't? Remember, the *métro* at

Chaussée-d'Antin; it is your key in and out of the 9ᵉ.

The Tenth (10ᵉ)

Wholesale, did you say you like wholesale? Well, the 10ᵉ is one of the many wholesale neighborhoods—this one is for furs, glass, china, and coiffure suppliers. The Saint-Denis area is filled with hookers. The 10ᵉ teems with renters seeking cheap shelter—hookers, dealers, hoods, etc. It has a strong ethnic mix as well. Not one of your must-see, must-write-home-about areas. Both the Gare du Nord and the Gare de l'Est are in the 10ᵉ.

The Eleventh (11ᵉ)

République is a middle-class neighborhood. We have some sources here for discounters, but mostly this is not a neighborhood you would go out of your way to shop in, simply because there is little that is special here. The furniture business stretches along the Rue du faubourg-Saint-Antoine, but it's not the kind of furniture you're looking for.

The Twelfth (12ᵉ)

This is Bastille–Gare de Lyon, which you might visit if you are a hot-to-trot tourist who has to see where Madame Defarge was knitting. The districts are: Bastille, Nation (partly in 20ᵉ), Reuilly, and Daumesnil.

The open market (Beauvau-Saint-Antoine) is at the Place d'Aligre, which is open every day except Monday until 1 P.M. and backs up on the covered market of the same name. The streets are filled with vendors selling fruit and veggies, flowers, and *fripes*. It's a very real-people neighborhood, not at all glamorous or quaint. But it's intensely French. We go here to visit Betty (page 125) and check out the *fripes*. There's a large Felix Potin grocery store here also; a covered market is around the corner on Rue d'Aligre.

The Thirteenth (13ᵉ)

One of the largest *arrondissements* of Paris, the 13ᵉ is mostly residential and of little interest to tourists; part of the area is known as the French Chinatown. The districts are: Italie, Gobelins, and Austerlitz.

The Fourteenth (14ᵉ)

We love the 14ᵉ because it is home to the Rue d'Alésia, a street of bargain shops. There's a good flea market here (Place de Vanves); Montparnasse is here if it interests you—in all its high-rise, Los Angeles–style glory. The neighborhood is large and has many districts—some are nice, others are not.

The Fifteenth (15ᵉ)

Shoppers of the world, unite: The 15ᵉ is yours if you come to Paris for *prêt*, or if you like to do half a day's bargain shopping. The Porte de Versailles is here, and there are tons of commercial streets all around. Rue de la Convention is a main drag. Mostly this is a middle-class, very respectable, almost chic, neighborhood.

The Sixteenth (16ᵉ)

To many Parisians there is only one *arrondissement* in Paris, and its number is 16. The districts are: Auteuil, Passy, Chaillot, Muette, and Porte Dauphine.

It just so happens that there are a few parts of the 16ᵉ that aren't chic (e.g., Port de Saint Cloud), but this is the seat of the BCBG (*bon chic, bon genre*), the FHCP (Foulard Hermès Collier de Perles), and the Nappy Society (named for the proper neighborhoods Neuilly, Auteuil, and Passy). What more could a yuppie want? Rue de Passy is the best commercial stretch of residential Paris. The 16ᵉ has its own park, the *Bois*, and it's very chic to live close to the park. More important, the 16ᵉ has lots of resale shops.

The Seventeenth (17ᵉ)

It's okay, Maman won't disown you if you live in the 17ᵉ (or parts of it, anyway). The acceptable districts for the BCBG group are: Péreire, Ternes, and Monceau.

The Eighteenth (18ᵉ)

You know the 18ᵉ because it includes the Montmartre neighborhood. Other districts in it are: Clignancourt, Pigalle, Chapelle, and Goutte-d'Or.

While the 18ᵉ was charming and famous and really cute for movies (*Irma la Douce*), books (*Mistral's Daughter*), and tourists (up to twenty years ago, anyway), now it is a less-than-charming place. The fabric markets of Saint-Pierre are near Sacré-Coeur.

The Nineteenth (19ᵉ)

This really is getting out of the swing of things; as you get to the Villette part of this *arrondissement* you are at the edge of the highway that encompasses Paris. The Villette market has closed down, so there's no reason to visit.

The Twentieth (20ᵉ)

Maurice Chevalier made the area famous when he sang about Ménilmontant, but other than that there isn't too much going on in this residential neighborhood inhabited by people who can't afford high rents in other parts of town. The famous Père-Lachaise cemetery is here; the only piece of retailing advice we have for this entire neighborhood is to make sure you buy a map of the gravestones; otherwise you will never find Jim Morrison's.

Trading Areas

We've gone through our travels thinking of certain shopping districts or even certain shopping blocks as "neighborhoods," knowing full well that they weren't really neighborhoods but not knowing what else to call them. Other people do the same thing, and retailers call these shopping neighborhoods trading areas. A trading area has no special boundaries, it moves and changes, and it is specific to a block, a plaza—even a shopping center. We do not attempt to list every store in a trading area; the names we have given these trading areas are strictly our own nicknames for them based on something that seemed obvious to us at the time.

Champs-Élysées

The first vision a schoolchild has of Paris usually includes the wide boulevard of the Champs-Élysées, crowned by L'Étoile and the Arc de Triomphe. It is perhaps the main drag of Paris. The Germans marched down it to make their

PARIS

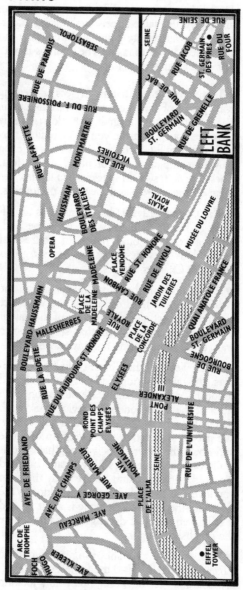

point quite clear; the Allies marched down it in delirious triumph. We have marched up and down the same street on shopping excursions for over twenty years, and we have a sad but honest report to make: The Champs-Élysées just isn't what it used to be.

▼ In summer, the Champs-Élysées is teeming with gangs of teenage boys of various ethnic backgrounds who, even if they don't overtly terrorize you, will make you so incredibly nervous that you'll take to the side streets or cling to your companion out of plain, simple fear. These boys travel in packs—you'll also see them on the *métro*—and they prey on tourists.

▼ The Champs-Élysées has changed as an address. While it used to be the very finest address a retailer could have—an address of tremendous prestige—now there are *degriffes* along the Champs-Élysées.

▼ While one of the great things about the Champs-Élysées used to be that you were safe walking there at almost any hour of the day or night, we do not suggest that single women walk there alone during nonbusiness hours.

▼ When we stroll the Champs-Élysées as shoppers, we take only one side of the boulevard seriously. Although there are stores on both sides of the street, one side obviously is much better. Usually we ignore the other side totally. We get no satisfaction in walking up one side and down the other. This is a long haul and is really boring—unless it's New Year's Eve and it's cold and crisp and you're with the man you love and the little lights are blinking in the trees and the Arc de Triomphe is all lit up and it is heaven and you don't give a damn where the good shopping is.

▼ The end of the shopping part of the Champs-Élysées is called the Rond Point. If you are standing at the Rond Point and looking straight ahead to the Arc de Triomphe, the good side of the street for shopping is on your right-hand side. You can begin at the YSL Rond Point or the shopping gallery called Galerie-Élysées Rond Point, which is a rather modern shopping mall not unlike one in your home city, except that it has only sixteen shops. There's a **CAREL** shoes (moderate prices), a **HEDIARD** (food, glorious food), a Hallmark shop (souvenirs), **ALAIN MANOUKIAN** (moderate sweaters), and a sculpted fountain of bronze fish that go around in a windmill.

▼ Along the way you'll see numerous car showrooms, perfume showrooms, drugstores, airlines offices, cafés, and change booths.

▼ Several big-name designers have stores here, such as **DANIEL HECHTER** at No. 50 and **TON SUR TON** at No. 82.

▼ Galerie du Claridge has two levels (go downstairs, too) and has the best selection among the kind of shops you want to see—most of them are big-name designers.

▼ There are several specialty stores that carry a lot of designers of the quality the French call *créateurs*—such as **CLAUDE MONTANA** and **BYBLOS**. In short, the hot names of fashion. **LIGHT**, at No. 92, is one such shop. Often buyers from the United States stop here to see what's hot and what's not.

▼ We're big Prisunic fans. **PRISUNIC** is a fancy dime store that was overhauled with the help of Andrée Putman, the famous interior designer who brought the store into the forefront of retailing and fashion in the 1960s. If you travel with your children, don't miss this location for cheap clothes, cheap toys, and the grocery store on the downstairs level. You also can buy Pampers here.

▼ We normally run across the street about when you get to **LE DRUGSTORE**, but you can walk past the *degriffes* and right up to the tomb of the Unknown Soldier.

▼ From Le Drugstore, we get off the Champs-Élysées and move into the couture side streets.

Victoires

We don't want to ruin the neighborhood by sending throngs of tourists here, but if you want to have a wonderful shopping experience that's very French and very safe, you'll forget the Champs-Élysées and go to Place des Victoires—which is nestled back into the area behind the Palais-Royal where the 1er and the 2e connect. The Place des Victoires is a plaza complete with a statue of a king on a horse. Facing the *place* is a circle of *hôtels*; the ground floor of each has been converted to retail space. The spokes of streets shooting out of the *place* represent various retail streets as well, and they are filling up with more and more wonderful shops. Rue Étienne-Marcel is the major drag—it has long housed some of the big *créateurs*. Going the other way is the Rue des Petits-Champs, which has a lot of showrooms and cutesy-pie shops on it. (The Galerie Vivienne is on the Rue des Petits-Champs right before the Place des Victoires.) Rue de Mail is gaining in popularity, but we take Rue d'Aboukir into the Sentier.

The anchor to Victoires is Kenzo, but this is not the kind of neighborhood where you go only into the shops you have heard about. Yes, there's **KENZO** and **CACHAREL**, but don't forget to try Victoires, another famous anchor to the neighborhood; **RICHARD TUIL** for Samurai; and **THIERRY MUGLER**. You will enjoy going door to door around the circle and then branching out down the little streets. It's OK to get lost and found here, since at worst you'll find another new shop.

Whether you opt for the Sentier tour or not, don't forget to check your trusty map before you leave Victoires; because the location is so superb, you can automatically segue into any of several different directions. The Galerie Vivienne is virtually one block away; you can easily walk to the Forum des Halles or to Opéra or the Boulevard Haussmann and the big department stores. You can also come around and hit Le Louvre des Antiquaires and then go to Benlux and the souvenir shops along the Rue de Rivoli—ending up at Concorde, or Place Vendôme, or on the Faubourg Saint-Honoré. The world starts at Victoires, and it's a magnificent world.

Sentier

Some people have printer's ink in their veins. We have garment center in our blood. We appreciate that not everyone does, so we exercise this warning right from the start. The Sentier may not be your kind of place. We can't imagine why you wouldn't like it, but that's because we like it so much. It's very much like New York's Seventh Avenue—men with pushcarts piled high with fabric, little showrooms that may or may not let you buy from them, hookers in certain doorways, junk in bins, metal racks and forklifts and hangers and mannequins without arms and all that stuff. There are few big-name designer names here, and there are no guarantees that you will find what you want.

One announcement: For the most part, the area is closed tight on weekends. A few shops are open on Saturday, but Saturday is not the day to tour the neighborhood and see it all. Sunday is totally dead.

Rue de Rivoli

The Rue de Rivoli is the main drag that runs along the back side of the Louvre. Since the Louvre once was a fortress, you will understand why it seems to go on forever. They just don't build them like that anymore. Exit the *métro* at Concorde. The Rue de Rivoli has many chic shops on it, including the newish **LANVIN 2,** the men's sport shop, and **HILDITCH & KEY.** As you pass the Inter•Continental (which has more stores in it than any other hotel in Paris) and the Meurice, you'll see more touristy stores, and the farther you go away from Concorde, the more touristy the stores will get. Just because a lot of tourists shop here doesn't mean this is a bad shopping area. Pick and choose at your own discretion. The trading area we call Rue de Rivoli ends at the Louvre des Antiquaires, but the street itself—Rue de Rivoli—continues forever and has many stores on it. By the time you get up near the Hôtel-de-Ville, there's the giant department store **BHV.** Some tourist must-do's:

W. H. SMITH, books in English, even if they don't carry our books, 248 Rue de Rivoli, 1er

BENLUX, three floors of duty-free semi-bargains. An excellent place for cosmetics and fragrance if you will not meet *détaxe* requirements, 174 Rue de Rivoli, 1er

The Left Bank

We have never known how to describe or tour the Left Bank adequately. Just go there and spend the day. No, just stay there and spend a week. Hmm—maybe you'd better move there.

To get a better grip on the whole thing, we divide it into four areas: Saint-Germain Main, Behind the Church, Rennes Central, and Little Dragons.

SAINT-GERMAIN MAIN

This is the main drag, on which the church by the same name is perched and where many people parade around to see and be seen. Many famous bistros are here, Le Drugstore is here, and Shu Uemura cosmetics is here. While there is a *métro* that comes out right next to the church, when we take a taxi all we say is "Le Drugstore Saint-Germain." That puts us right smack in the center of the neighborhood, a good starting point from which to explore on foot.

BEHIND THE CHURCH

In front of the church of Saint-Germain-des-Prés you always will find street merchants. When the other stores are closed, the street merchants are open, especially on summer evenings, when it doesn't get dark until 10 P.M. Behind the church you'll find: Place de Furstemberg, Rue de Buci, Rue Jacob, Rue Bonaparte, Rue de Seine, Rue du Bac, and Quai Voltaire.

These streets are filled mostly with antiques shops, bakeries, eateries, markets, and restaurants (see page 188 for antiques). It is very quaint back here, and the stores feel different from the ones in the other parts of the Left Bank. This is one of the most charming areas in all of Paris.

RENNES CENTRAL

Across the street from the church there's a Le Drugstore and a point where two streets converge in a V—the Rue de Rennes and the Rue Bonaparte. Bonaparte runs behind the church as well; Rennes does not. Rennes is the central drag of this trading area, which includes such streets as: Rue de Seine, Rue de Tournon, Rue Saint-Sulpice, Rue Coétlogon, and Boulevard Raspail.

This area doesn't feel quite as cozy as the part behind the church; there are fewer antiques shops and more boutiques for ready-to-wear and designer goods. Saint Laurent gave the neighborhood its big push when he opened on Saint-Sulpice. Rennes—sort of a main drag with a **CÉLINE**, **CHARLES JOURDAN**, etc.—is far more commercial than Rue de Seine and Rue de Tournon. The quainter part of this neighborhood often is called Odéon by locals. Don't miss:

SOULEIADO, the original Pierre Deux, 78 Rue de Seine

WALTER STEIGER, exquisite, expensive designer shoes, Rue de Tournon

LAURA ASHLEY, who else but? 94 Rue de Rennes

JOSEPH TRICOT, snazzy British designer, 70 Rue Bonaparte

LA BAGAGERIE, luggage and handbags, good savings on U.S. prices, 41 Rue du Four

RIVE GAUCHE, YSL's men's and women's shops, 6 and 12 Rue Saint-Sulpice

LITTLE DRAGONS

To the right of Rennes Central are several very small, narrow little streets crammed with good things to eat and to wear. They are epitomized by the Rue du Dragon, the heart of this area, which is why we call this neighborhood Little Dragons. Then there're Rue de Grenelle and Rue des Saints-Pères.

If you follow the Rue de Grenelle, a street worth following, it will take you to Invalides and another trading area. Along the way, try:

SONIA RYKIEL, three designer boutiques, 4–6–8 Rue de Grenelle

EMILIA, stunning leather shoes and handbags, 9 Rue de Grenelle

MAUD FRIZON, shoes, dear; handbags are in another store around the corner, 83 Rue des Saints-Pères

PRADA, handbags, shoes, nylon totes, currently very "in," 5 Rue de Grenelle

WORKSHOP (YOHJI YAMAMOTO), *le dernier cri Japonais,* 4 Rue du Dragon

XAVIER DANAUD, moderately priced but hip shoes; Jourdan last, 78 Rue des Saints-Pères

Place Vendôme

If you're looking for a neighborhood that says "Paris" and reminds you with every breath that they don't make 'em like this anymore, get yourself over to the Place Vendôme, conveniently located between Opéra and Rue de Rivoli.

Formerly one of the finest residential areas in Paris, the Place Vendôme is surrounded by *hôtels* that now are either jewelry shops, banks, insurance companies, or all three. There's also a hotel of the type you spend the night in—the Ritz. Besides the big jewelry firms, like **VAN CLEEF AND ARPELS** at No. 22 and **CARTIER** at No. 13, some ready-to-wear kings have moved in—like **GIORGIO ARMANI** at No. 6 and **NATORI** at No. 7.

The far side of the Place Vendôme is the Rue de la Paix, which dead-ends into Opéra. There are more jewelers here (and even a **BURMA** if you like to buy copies of what you have just seen), and a few other retailers. Don't confuse **CHARVET** (a men's store) with **CHAUMET**—a jeweler. The American Express office is on Rue Scribe, right beside Opéra.

Haussmann

On the other side of Opéra, and the other side of the world from Place Vendôme, is the Boulevard Haussmann, where several department stores have their headquarters. This three-block-long and two-block-deep jumble of merchandise, pushcarts, strollers, and shoppers is a central trading area. We often refer to it as the Zoo. If you insist on seeing it, go early in the morning (10 A.M.), when you are strong. Winter is far less zoolike than summer.

Passy

We don't want to build Passy out of proportion; it is merely the main commercial street of one of the nicest districts of one of the nicest *arrondissements* of Paris. It has a little of everything and is convenient to other neighborhoods; you can visit Passy and go on your way to the Tour Eiffel, to Trocadero, to the resale shops of the 16ᵉ, or you can catch the *métro* and be anywhere else in minutes. Passy is in transition, but it has some old faithfuls tucked between the overly commercial ones and offers an excellent chance to see some of the real Paris ... and to get to Sephora, a wonderful makeup store.

As you stroll, don't miss:

PASSY DEGRIFFE, moderate sportswear and work clothes, $25 to $75, 15 Rue de Passy, 16ᵉ

REAL, branch of the designer digs, 16 Rue de Passy, 16ᵉ

PRISUNIC, our favorite dime store in the world, Rue de Passy, 16ᵉ

LES OLIVADES, a competitor of Souleiado's in back of Inno, 25 Rue de L'Annonciation, 16ᵉ

INNO, a far classier version of Prisunic; don't forget the supermarket downstairs, 54 Rue de Passy, 16ᵉ

SEPHORA, cosmetics, cosmetics, cosmetics, cosmetics, 50 Rue de Passy, 16ᵉ

NADINE SAMPSON, Junko Koshino, Alaïa, Miss V, etc., 58 Rue de Passy, 16ᵉ

FRANCK ET FILS, small department store of tremendous elegance with couture selection and big-name designers, 80 Rue de Passy, 16ᵉ

COQUELIN AINÉ, tearoom, lunch stop, chocolate macaroons, 67 Rue de Passy, 16ᵉ

Bastille

Don't look now, but Bastille is getting to be chic. Dare we say it? People are losing their heads over this up-and-coming neighborhood! A tad too far uptown for general retail, Bastille is benefiting from the rebirth of the Marais, one *arrondissement* over, and the anniversary of the French Revolution. The artists have moved in; so have the Americans (to live, not to set up shop), and with the new Bastille Opéra, it's all uphill. Long known as the basic home furnishings area, the district is now taking on some galleries and interior design shops of note. For a snack, or tea, or a drink, or to watch the world go by, stop at La Tour d'Argent at 6 Place de la Bastille or at the long-famous *brasserie,* Bofinger, at 5 Rue de la Bastille. To see it all, take the *métro* to Ledru-Rollin and walk along the Rue Saint-Antoine toward the column in the center of the Place de la Bastille. Don't forget that there's the **JEAN-LOUIS SCHERRER** discount shop at 29 Avenue Ledru-Rollin, right near this *métro* stop. If you are not interested in home decorating, you can probably pass. On the other side of the *place,* pass Bofinger and move to more shopping on the Rue Saint-Antoine where the discount houses begin, like **AT EASE DEGRIFFES** (22 Rue Saint-Antoine), or jeans shops like **DANIEL**, at Nos. 38, 42, 44, and 68 Rue Saint-Antoine. You can follow the signs to the Place des Vosges from here, you can visit the antiques market around Saint Paul, or you can walk straight to the Hôtel de Ville. Rue Saint-Antoine becomes the Rue de Rivoli, so you could actually walk all the way back to the Meurice.

Marais/Place des Vosges

The rebirth of the Marais is not a new song these days, but new shops are still showing up, so the area becomes a pleasure to explore each time you visit Paris. Take the *métro* to Saint Paul and follow the signs. If you love the out-of-the-way and special, stay at the Pavillon de la Reine (see page 12), which is built where the former queen's chambers once were, in the style of the 14th century—it's a true find. Take in designer shops like **POPY MORENI** (No. 13), and **FANNY** (No. 21) for *fripes,* as you roam the square, then take off into the side streets. You're near the Rue de Turenne, which has absolutely no charm whatsoever and will ruin the mood, but which has a ton of jobbers and discount shops (**BIDERMAN**, No. 114), and the Rue du Temple, which is another street of discounters; in between them are quaint little streets and shops you've never heard of before that will bring a smile to your face and your pocketbook. Try **ANDRE BISSONÉT** (6 Rue du Pas-de-la-Mule), who has an amazing collection of antique musical instruments; **À LA BONNE RENOMMÉE** (26 Rue Vieille du Temple), which sells very expensive patchwork fashions; **AUTOUR DU MONDE** (12 Rue des Francs Bourgeois) which is the French version of Banana Republic! Continuing on Rue des Francs Bourgeois, there's **LEFAX** for Filofax goodies in French (No. 32) right nearby; **MONIC**, for glitzy fun jewelry (No. 5); and **JEAN PIERRE DE CASTO** (No. 17) for silver and silverplate sold by weight. Of course, there's **PATRICK KELLY**, the wild and crazy American from Mississippi who is the toast of the town (6 Rue du Parc Royal), and **AZZEDINE ALAÏA**, the wild and crazy Frenchman from North Africa, also the toast of the town (17 Rue du Parc Royal).

Don't forget the side streets near the Picasso Museum, where there are many trendy shops.

Alésia

Pronounced "Aleeeza" by some and "heaven" by us, this is one of the major discount districts in Paris. Prices in some of these shops may not be the lowest possible, but the assortment is spectacular, and it's all here for you. *Tip*: Not every store in this area is a discount house, so ask if you are confused. Don't make any false assumptions! Most of the discount houses have the word *stock* in their name, which means they sell overruns. There are three such "stock" shops for **DOROTHÉE BIS** (at Nos. 74, 76, and 78 Rue d'Alésia), and then there's our favorite of them all, **STOCK2** (No. 92), which is a warehouse kind of place that feels as nice as a department store and sells men's, women's, and kids' designer clothes at discount prices. Most of it is from Daniel Hechter, but there are other brands. Don't miss **CACHAREL STOCK** (No. 114) and **LE GRAND MAGASIN D'USINE CENTER** (No. 120). Alésia is in the 14e, which is also the district for the Vanves flea market, held on Saturdays and Sundays. You can make quite a day of it on a Saturday, should you be half mad and love crowds.

Saint-Placide

This is not particularly near Alésia (although we've walked to it), but mentally the two areas are sisters—homes of the discount shop, the "stock" shop, the great bargain. Saint-Placide is a side street that is right alongside Bon Marché, the department store on the Left Bank. Take the *métro* to Saint-Placide and walk toward Bon Marché. Along the Saint-Placide you'll pass about twenty "stock" shops, from the cheap junk type to the designer type. **DIS-**

COUNT R stands for Real, a well-known French designer with a few shops now in the United States (No. 37); **MAGIC SOLDES** sells children's clothes (No. 60)—it's a rather large chain, so you might want to find their other addresses, which are mostly suburban; **L'ANNEXE** (No. 48) carries some designer things. Try **COMME DES FEMMES** (No. 31) for lingerie; Stock (three shops: Nos, 26, 30, and 51) sells Caroll knits and overruns; and **KING SOLDES** has all sorts of things but has never been overrun with familiar names (No. 24). Our favorite shop of the whole street is **LE MOUTON À 5 PATTES** (No. 48), where we lucked into designer kids' clothes at incredibly cheap prices. Clothes for grown-ups, even designer clothes for grown-ups, have been spotted here.

Sainte-Placide feels a bit seedy and isn't as attractive as Alésia, but there's nothing wrong with the neighborhood, and it is safe. Walk along the street choosing what interests you until you come head-on to the Rue de Sèvres, which is a main drag for real-people shopping. Because **BON MARCHÉ** is right there, many other retailers have come along with branch stores to catch the overflow department-store traffic. There's a **GUERLAIN** and **RODIER** and **DOROTHÉE BIS** and a lot of nice stores. It is not fancy here, but quite serviceable. You're also at the corner of the Hôtel Concorde-Lutetia, where you can explore the lobby and use the bathroom. There is a *métro* in the square (Sèvres-Babylone), or you can take the Rue de Sèvres for one block and hit the really exciting, fancy, expensive stores of the area we call Little Dragons—the Left Bank's best boutiques are right here on Rue de Grenelle and the adjoining streets. Stop for oysters at Bistro Lutetia.

Saint-Honoré

Most shoppers have heard of the famous Rue du faubourg-Saint-Honoré, the street where most of the fancy designer shops—and many of the world's fanciest antiques shops—are located. What they don't know is that the word *faubourg* usually indicates a small street, leading off a street with the same name that is bigger. The Rue du faubourg-Saint-Honoré actually extends from the Rue Saint-Honoré, which stretches quite some distance, and is crammed with shops. We also recommend plain old Saint-Honoré, especially in the area we call Behind the Meurice. This is a part of town tourists don't usually see, but it is the typical example of how real (but rich) French people live and shop. You'll find little shops, especially service shops like grocers and butchers and shoemakers and bakeries, and the area market, as well as a few unexpected treats— discounters as well as couturiers. One of our secret stops: La Table Gourmande (6 Rue du Marché Saint-Honoré), a tiny *traiteur* with take-out food—you can eat a wonderful meal for $5. There's no place to sit down, so go to the park for a picnic or return to your hotel room, if you are staying nearby.

To find this hidden area, when you get to the Rue Royale, where the *faubourg* ends and the regular Rue Saint-Honoré begins, just keep on walking on Rue Saint-Honoré, going up-town toward the Palais-Royal. You'll pass a good number of designer shops like **LACOSTE** (No. 372) and **MCM** (No. 243), and fun, funky stores like **ANEMONE** (No. 235) and **ANCOLIE** (No. 233), and then get to the Marché Saint-Honoré, a fabulous small street that is one block long and leads you right to the covered market, passing all kinds of good food shops and a fine source for discount shoes—**GIGI**, 30 Place du Marché Saint-Honoré. On the other side of the Marché are **CASTELBAJAC** (No. 31) and **PHILIPPE MODEL** (No. 33).

Étienne-Marcel

Étienne-Marcel isn't really a neighborhood. It's a street right in the middle of one of our favorite neighborhoods: it connects Victoires to the Forum des Halles and borders the Sentier, the wholesale district of Paris. But we are drawing your attention to it because it's one of the most fun streets in Paris and has such a special feel to it that you imagine it to be an entity unto itself. Several designers have built shops here, the kind of shops you see pictured in architectural magazines. There's the **GIRBAUD** shop (No. 38), which is called **HALLES CAPONE**; a **JOSEPH TRICOT** shop (No. 44); **COMME DES GARÇONS** (No. 42); **YOHJI YAMA-MOTO** (No. 47); and **JUNKO SHIMADA** (No. 54). There is a *métro* called Étienne-Marcel that will bring you right here, but we really would prefer that you take the *métro* to Bourse, take in the Place des Victoires, and then walk along Étienne-Marcel until you connect to the Forum des Halles. When you see the *métro* at Rue Turbigo, turn right and prowl the shops here (designer and discount) and then walk one block into the new part of the Forum at its Les Halles entrance.

La Défense

La Défense is not a neighborhood for tourists, but should be filed in the back of your mind for the time when you swap houses with a French family and move to Paris for a few weeks. La Défense is a high-rise business section in Courbevoie, a suburb of Paris, but along with the businesses there is a huge shopping area with a *hypermarché* (supermarket) and many resources for inexpensive and fun household and life-style items. This is for French yuppies who bring the car and load up on Saturdays. If you want to see how the real people do it, this is modern French sociological shopping—American style!

Palais des Congrès (Porte Maillot)

If you aren't going to La Défense on business, your business may have you a prisoner at the Palais des Congrès, the big convention center that is most famous because it is where the airport bus drops you off. Not scenic, but there are a lot of stores here (over eighty of them)—many are branches of designer shops like **CHARLES JOURDAN**, **LOUIS FERAUD**, **CHRISTIAN DIOR**, **PIERRE CARDIN**, **DANIEL HECHTER**, **ANDRÉ COURRÈGES**, etc. Get a Japanese luncheon snack at **DAIMARU**, a branch of the Tokyo (and Hong Kong) department store. The shopping mall is lacking in ambience but the opportunities to spend are many.

6 ▾ LE SHOPPING

Continental Big Names

Despite the fact that the French think French fashion is the best in the world (many other people happen to agree), they have allowed other designers and resources to open up shop in the City of Light. Of course, the Italians have a good number of shops, representing some of the most famous names in fashion. And many of the world's big fashion names come from other countries yet show their lines in Paris (Per Spook, Valentino, Hanae Mori), and so are considered French designers. Kenzo may have been born in Japan, but there is no question that he is considered a French designer. Paris has recently gone crazy for the American look (see page 83). Many U.S. designers have chosen to make it in Paris (Patrick Kelly) or to open branch and *branche* shops.

LAURA ASHLEY: The French think that the English schoolgirl is acceptably BCBG, so there are eight Ashley shops (if you count the designer showrooms).

If you have a business card, you can buy paint and wallcovering from the showroom— but you will not get *détaxe* and must await delivery. If you buy the same items retail, you will get the same discount that designers get in the form of your *détaxe* and have immediate delivery. We don't know if you like the notion of schlepping a suitcase filled with wallpaper halfway around the world, but we've done it to great satisfaction and savings. Laura Ashley, like all European wall coverings, comes in *double* rolls—so make sure you have the right count before you buy.

LAURA ASHLEY
94 Rue de Rennes, 6ᵉ (Métro: Rennes)
261 Rue Saint-Honoré, 1ᵉʳ (Métro: Concorde)
95 Avenue Raymond Poincaré, 16ᵉ (Métro: Victor Hugo)
Also boutiques in Galeries Lafayette and Au Printemps.

LAURA ASHLEY SHOWROOM, 34 Rue de Grenelle, 6ᵉ (Métro: Bac)

▼

GIORGIO ARMANI: Even if you can't afford to buy Armani, you can afford to walk over to the Place Vendôme and stalk through this store. It is one of the most magnificent pieces of architecture you'll see on the retail scene, anywhere in the world. The sleek, tailored clothes, for both men and women, are displayed as if in a temple. The Place Vendôme has heretofore been home mostly to the biggest names in jewelry, but Armani, as always, has started a trend.

GIORGIO ARMANI, 6 Place Vendôme, 1ᵉʳ (Métro: Tuileries)

▼

BOTTEGA VENETA: Bottega in Paris is cheaper than in the United States but may not be the bargain you were hoping for. They do have huge sales in January and in July, and then you can really clean up. *Détaxe* will make your bargain that much more appealing. Don't forget to check out the downstairs.

BOTTEGA VENETA, 48 Avenue Victor Hugo, 16ᵉ (Métro: Victor Hugo)

▼

CERUTTI 1881: Nino Cerutti is the Italian designer of this line, which has become a European staple for well-dressed men who fancy the lean, narrow look and the more-elegant-than-thou color choices. Not for big American bodies or small-town tastes, but otherwise one of the most dashing lines in the world.

CERUTTI 1881, 15 Place de la Madeleine, 8ᵉ (Métro: Madeleine)

▼

ESCADA: New to Paris, this German line offers expensive sportswear to the French, who adore the look of elegant separates that have a sporty tone with a dressy appeal. You can look casually rich when done up in Escada, but never BCBG. The shop is bordered by polished brass and offers a nice setting for the wares of this international chain. No bargains.

ESCADA, 418 Rue Saint-Honoré, 8ᵉ (Métro: Concorde)

▼

GUCCI: We have found at least three Gucci stores in Paris, so be advised that the big, easy-to-spot Gucci on the corner of the Rue du faubourg-Saint-Honoré is not the only shops in town. We found the nicest Gucci salespeople in the world in the main shop, as well as a tremendous amount of merchandise that we hadn't seen in Italy. Prices are quite reasonable on the basics.

Gucci is one of those lines, especially when it comes to accessories, that is sold in many of the snazzy "duty free" shops that are concentrated in the tourist shopping areas. The shops will make you think they are discounting the Gucci price on top of the *détaxe* reduction, when we've never found a shop that really gives the discount; or they will tell you that they have special merchandise you can't find anywhere else. While there is a huge discrepancy in merchandise from Gucci to Gucci and from country to country, the basic items are almost universally available.

GUCCI

27 Rue de faubourg-Saint-Honoré, 8ᵉ (Métro: Concorde)
21 Rue Royale, 8ᵉ (Métro: Concorde)
350 Rue Saint-Honoré, 1ᵉʳ (Métro: Concorde)

▼

JAEGER PF FRANCE: Jaeger is so unmistakably English that it makes us chuckle to think of buying it in Paris—but the large, easy-to-shop store is right on the Rue du faubourg-Saint-Honoré, and does a huge business. Designed and furnished exactly like most of the American stores, the Paris Jaeger has prices only slightly higher than in London, and has the exact same clothes we saw in the United States for the same time period. Which is not something we can say about many famous boutiques. Expect to pay 25% less than the American retail price, with *détaxe* adding to your savings.

JAEGER PF FRANCE, 5 Rue du faubourg-Saint-Honoré, 8ᵉ (Métro: Concorde)

▼

KRIZIA: Italian best-dressed genius Mariuccia Mandelli has brought Krizia to Paris in a large shop that lets the world know she's a contender for your hard-earned savings. The Moods line is made in Hong Kong for The Limited, and is not sold in this Krizia shop or any other; the Poi line is a little less expensive than the regular couture line. Prices here are very high, but the look has a certain way of letting the world know that the wearer is exciting, original, and ahead of the times.

KRIZIA, 27 Rue du faubourg-Saint-Honoré, 1er (Métro: Concorde)

▼

MISSONI: Very modern and fun, the Missoni shop in Paris is more comfortable (and comforting) than the flagship store in Milan. The prices are about 20% higher than in Italy, but still will give you a savings if you are a Missoni nut. They have two excellent sales, in July and January—so you may want to wait for them. Even with the benefit of a strong dollar, lower European prices, and going without lunch for six months, we find Missoni still is expensive. Look across the street at T. J. Vestor for Missoni bed linens.

MISSONI, 43 Rue du Bac, 7e (Métro: Bac)

▼

TRUSSARDI: The Trussardi shop in Paris is a few paces from the Élysées Palace, and is a palace of its own sort. It feels like a converted town house but was just a little private manse, in years gone by. Trussardi have painted the floors gray, used stark white on the walls, and done a wonderful job of showing off both their clothes and leather luggage goods in this spacious outlet. They have one of the best selections of goods in the world (we even like this store better than the ones in Italy); prices are only slightly higher than in Italy and are really quite reasonable for this kind of status canvas and leather.

TRUSSARDI, 77 Rue du faubourg-Saint-Honoré, 8e (Métro: Miromesnil)

▼

STEFANEL: No, Stefanel is not owned by Benetton, although the look is similar. Stefanel is more sophisticated in color and style. Several of these Italian knitwear specialty shops have sprung up in Paris, attracting a more upscale version of the Benetton client.

STEFANEL, 18 Rue Royale, 8ᵉ (Métro: Madeleine)

▼

ERMENEGILDO ZEGNA: If you want to spend a lot of money and take on the suave, sophisticated look of a modern Count of Monte Cristo, do not miss Zegna, which is just becoming well-known in the United States (through some new shops), but has been known for centuries in Europe, as the maker of the world's finest wools. The Zegna family runs the mills that always have provided the best designers with their wool. Just recently they have begun a men's ready-to-wear line. A wool jacket or tailored suit from Zegna tells the world that you have arrived. Ladies, bring the man you love here. Above any French big name, we suggest you give serious consideration to this Italian big name. Prices range from $100 to $1,000.

ERMENEGILDO ZEGNA, 10 Rue de la Paix, 1ᵉʳ (Métro: Opéra)

American Big Names

The second American liberation of Paris began quietly enough when Ralph Lauren opened a shop right at Place de la Madeleine. Now American designers are hustling to open doors to sell more than the American look previously defined as a pair of Levi's. You can see this merchandise (except for Patrick Kelly's works) at home, and pay less for it, so here's a brief blow-by-blow of the Americans in Paris:

RALPH LAUREN/POLO: It's all here, just like on Madison Avenue: the fancy woodwork, the gorgeous antiques, the overripe roses in the Chinese porcelain bowl. Men's clothing is downstairs, women's and children's is upstairs. Americans need visit only if they need a laugh—the prices here are so expensive that it makes regular Ralph at retail look like a bargain.

RALPH LAUREN/POLO, 2 Place de la Madeleine, 8e (Métro: Madeleine)

▼

PATRICK KELLY: Kelly moved to Paris from Mississippi and made it big with buttons and bows. He has deals with Benetton and with Warnaco who manufacture an American line that he designs from Paris. But there is a French collection as well. The French clothes are young and zippy and a tad ridiculous, and not wearable by anyone we know, but are highly inventive and imaginative and colorful and fun.

PATRICK KELLY, 6 Rue du Parc Royal, 3e (Métro: Saint-Paul)

▼

JOSIE NATORI: The queen of American underwear is actually Filipino, but she makes the most luxurious looks we've ever hankered after, and has developed enough of an international following to take on the French, who certainly appreciate fine underwear.

JOSIE NATORI, 7 Place Vendôme, 1er (Métro: Tuileries)

WILLIWEAR: Despite the death of designer Willi Smith, his company keeps on tackling the world and winning. Stores have opened in London and Paris, and continue to attract local fans. Willi Smith was the first person to create casual, moderately priced but fashionable sportswear. No wonder his clothes are so popular in France.

WILLIWEAR, 92 Rue de Richelieu, 2ᵉ (Métro: Bourse)

▼

JOAN & DAVID: Straight from your favorite Ann Taylor store, Joan and David the shoe people have become Joan and David the clothes people. They took over the Rayne shoe store right smack in the middle of Paris's prime shopping area; so they really want you to know that the Americans have landed. Needless to say, the prices here are for the rich, rich, rich.

JOAN & DAVID, 6 Rue du faubourg-Saint-Honoré, 8ᵉ (Métro: Concorde)

French Big Names

DOROTHÉE BIS: The woman responsible for getting this business off the ground was none other than the Duchess of Windsor. Sweaters and knits always have been the house specialty, and continue as such. Prices are moderate to those of us used to outrageously high designer prices. There are several retail outlets, but we like the one in the Forum des Halles. They have absolutely fabulous sales here—the kind where they throw things in bins and mark them $5. Drool, drool. There's also a boutique in Galeries Lafayette.

Then again, if you can't wait for the sale, drop by Dorothée Bis Stock for markdowns and leftovers. The shopowner takes great pride in having the best of the "stock" shops on the Rue d'Alésia, and she marks the clothes down progressively to get rid of them. Don't forget to check out the active sportswear. The ski clothes are fab-u-lous. Sometimes you can find children's (girls') clothes here as well.

Don't forget Dorotennis, which sometimes is a separate shop and sometimes is attached to a Dorothée Bis shop—it's (can you guess?) an active sportswear shop.

DOROTHÉE BIS
Forum des Halles, 1ᵉʳ (Métro: Châtelet)
33 Rue de Sèvres, 6ᵉ (Métro: Sèvres-Babylone)
DOROTHÉE BIS STOCK, 76 Rue d'Alésia, 14ᵉ
(Métro: Alésia)

▼

CACHAREL: Jean Cacharel made his name in America when he introduced sweet clothes in Liberty of London prints. Thankfully he has graduated from sweet along with the rest of us, and now does a wide line of separates that are moderately priced. We think the sale prices in the United States are great, and you may not be able to do better pricewise in Europe. For our money, Cacharel is a fabulous resource for children's clothes rather than adult fashion. But that's just our opinion. A suit for a little boy may cost over $100, but it's the kind of suit that should be worn for the family Christmas portrait.

The full range (but a season old) also is carried at Cacharel Stock, where prices run about half of French retail.

CACHAREL
34 Rue Tronchet, 8ᵉ (Métro: Madeleine)
5 Place des Victoires, 1ᵉʳ (Métro: Bourse)
CACHAREL STOCK
114 Rue d'Alésia, 14ᵉ (Métro: Alésia)

▼

PIERRE CARDIN: Pierre Cardin has so many shops in Paris, owns so many fabulous outlets to his creativity (including Maxim's), and licenses so many goods that it's impossible to tell you where to shop for his things. There are a few boutiques alone on the Faubourg-Saint-Honoré. There is Maxim's and an elegant men's shop next door on the Rue Royale. Another shop on Victor Hugo. And the beat goes on.

The outlet store at Sebastopol sells men's suits at discount. If you look at the building directory, however, you'll see the listing for Pierre Cardin and can proceed to the third floor. When you walk through the doorway you will have one of those queer sensations that asks, "Am I in the right place?" Push on. It's worth it. The man sitting at the desk does not speak English, nor is he particularly a salesman. In the sparsely furnished rooms you enter you will see boxes shipped from all over the world from various Pierre Cardin shops that have returned merchandise.

PIERRE CARDIN, 27 Avenue Victor Hugo, 16ᵉ (Métro: Victor Hugo)
PIERRE CARDIN PRESTIGE, 29 Rue du faubourg-Saint-Honoré (Métro: Concorde)
PIERRE CARDIN SOLDES, 11 Boulevard de Sebastopol, 3rd floor, 1ᵉʳ; hours: Monday to Saturday, 9:15 A.M. to 1 P.M., 2 P.M. to 6:30 P.M. (Métro: Châtelet)

▼

JEAN CHARLES DE CASTELBAJAC: Our enthusiasm for this avant-garde designer is immense. If your hotel is nearby (as are the Meurice, Inter•Continental, Lotti, and Ritz) and you always stroll nearby, you will enjoy this little pocket of fashion where several designers have found their niche. Otherwise Castelbajac may be too wild and too expensive for you to make the special trip. Of course, if you even know who we are talking about you must like this man—so step this way. Prices from $300.

CASTELBAJAC, 31 Place du marché Saint-Honoré, 1er (Métro: Tuileries)

▼

CHANEL: There's not much to say about Chanel that you don't already know, haven't read, or haven't seen on the Broadway stage. Now that Karl Lagerfeld is designing the line, it's even more fun than it was before. The Rue Cambon shop is the couture house and main shop. It's conveniently right behind the Ritz Hotel on a very inconspicuous part of the Rue Cambon. Two small boutiques are open across town.

There aren't a lot of bargains here, even on sale. A lot of the accessories are put away in black cases, so you have to ask to be shown the earrings and chains, which is no fun and puts a lot of pressure on you. We were looking for $50 earrings, which are possible to find but take some looking (average price: $75 to $150).

If you're game, we suggest a *used* Chanel suit. A classic is a classic is a classic, no? Check with Réciproque or Didier Ludot. Used suits are not cheap, since this is not a new trick. You'll pay about $500 for a good suit. Usually the blouse is sold with the suit at Ludot; at Chanel the blouse is another purchase.

One of our best sources for discount Chanel suits is in Italy, so check out Roland in Rome, right on the Spanish Steps. These may be excellent copies, or the real thing with different labels; we can't tell.

CHANEL

31 Rue Cambon, 1er (Métro: Tuileries)

42 Avenue Montaigne, 8e (Métro: F. D. Roosevelt)

6–8 Avenue Victor Hugo, 16e (Métro: Victor Hugo)

DIDIER LUDOT, 24 Galerie Montpensier, Jardin du Palais-Royal, 1er (Métro: Palais-Royal)

▼

CHARVET: Although Charvet sells both men's and women's clothing, this is known as one of the grandest resources for men in Continental Europe. Elegant men have been having shirts tailored here for centuries. You may buy off the rack, or bespoke. Off the rack comes only with one sleeve length, so big American men may need bespoke. The look is very Brooks Brothers; the minidepartment store of a shop is filled with *boiserie* and the look of old money. A man's shirt is going to cost over $100, and some people will tell you it's worth it (we won't, but others will).

CHARVET, 8 Place Vendôme, 1er (Métro: Opéra)

▼

COMME DES GARÇONS: This Euro-Japanese look is far more Japanese (as is its designer) and artistic than French and wearable, but designers and buyers like to look at the line for its avant-garde notions. We don't know anyone who drives in a car pool in Westport wearing these clothes. Expensive but exciting.

COMME DES GARÇONS, 42 Rue Étienne-Marcel, 2e (Métro: Étienne-Marcel)

▼

ANDRÉ COURRÈGES: Courrèges has a very traditional basic line, some dynamite skiwear, and very little that is weird or wacky. You still can find some stuff that is so reminiscent of the 1970s that you don't know if it's new or old merchandise, but there are no little white vinyl boots around. There is a boutique at

Galeries Lafayette and several other boutiques in various parts of Paris.

We find discounts, however, at 7 Rue Turbigo. The merchandise is out of season, but what else is new? The basic knits are classics.

ANDRÉ COURRÈGES

7 Rue Turbigo, 1er (Métro: Étienne-Marcel)

46 Rue du faubourg-Saint-Honoré, 8e (Métro: Concorde)

40 Rue François, 1er, 8e (Métro: F. D. Roosevelt)

▼

PIERRE DEUX/SOULEIADO: You have to be a real Pierre Deux freak to know that Charles Demery is the man who designs all those *provençal* prints we adore or to know that Pierre Deux is the name of the American franchise for those prints but *is not* the name of the company in Europe. So remember the word Souleiado—which will get you through France—and remember that the line is sold under different names in different parts of the world.

There are thirty-seven Souleiados in France alone (nineteen U.S. Pierre Deux; three shops in Tokyo) and three Souleiado shops in Paris—we hate even to tell you about the one in the Forum des Halles, because it pales compared to the Left Bank shop. The Rue de Seine shop, the *great* shop, is everything it should be. Next door but around the corner to it is the professional showroom, by the way. You will be in Country French heaven. Be sure to see all parts of the shop (there are two separate rooms); the consumer shop winds around a bit to what looks like another showroom in the far back, where more fabrics are sold by the meter.

We asked Souleiado if they would take our order on the phone from the United States and ship to us. They immediately responded that they certainly would not—if we wanted to buy in the United States we should go to a Pierre Deux shop!

SOULEIADO

78 Rue de Seine, 6ᵉ (Métro: Mabillon)
Forum des Halles, 1ᵉʳ (Métro: Châtelet)
85 Avenue Paul-Doumer, 16ᵉ (Métro: Muette)

▼

CHRISTIAN DIOR: Although the real Christian Dior is dead, the line carries on his fashionable tradition as designed by Marc Bohan. The large house has many floors for shopping—you can get ready-to-wear, costume jewelry, cosmetics, scarves, menswear, baby items, and wedding gifts as well as the couture. In fact, several little shops are clustered around the main "house."

One of the best things about the House of Dior is that they seem quite aware that you want to buy from them and have gone out of their way to have items priced for tourists with taste. The gift department is exhaustive—local brides often register here. There are numerous $25–$50 items that will be gift-wrapped for you in the ever-distinctive wrappings that will make your gift list wilt with delight. We give Dior high marks for merchandising their famous name to make everyone happy.

CHRISTIAN DIOR, 30 Avenue Montaigne, 8ᵉ (Métro: Alma Marceau)

▼

JEAN-PAUL GAULTIER: Difficult decision —to buy Gaultier in Milan, where the shop is easily accessible, or to go out of the way in Paris (well, not too far out of the way) and get the *détaxe*. The Paris shop is fun and worth seeing—turn-of-the-century (last century, silly) charm is mixed with videotech to show off the master of weird's no-longer-so-weird designs.

A belt still will set you back $200 or more. Be sure to walk into the Galerie Vivienne, which is behind this shop.

JEAN-PAUL GAULTIER, 6 Rue Vivienne, 2ᵉ (Métro: Bourse)

▼

MARITHE ET FRANÇOIS GIRBAUD: Masters of the Unisex look, the Girbauds still are making the only clothes that make sense on either sex with equal style.

The discount shop (beyond the courtyard) has strange hours, but the selection can be very good and very cheap. Pants are about $30. What's especially wonderful about the line is its unisex appeal. You are also more likely to fit into a variety of sizes, since the clothes are meant to be oversize. Not all sizes are always on hand at the discount division, but it's worth a try if you find yourself in the neighborhood. There is another discount out-let (Le Mouton à 5 Pattes) two doors away from the Left Bank shop, at 6 Rue Saint-Placide.

MARITHE ET FRANÇOIS GIRBAUD, 38 Rue Étienne-Marcel, 1ᵉʳ (Métro: Étienne-Marcel)
DROLES DE CHOSE POUR DROLES DE GENS, 14 Rue des Colonnes-du-Trône, 12ᵉ. Hours: Monday, Wednesday, Friday, and Satur-day, 2 P.M. to 7 P.M. (Métro: Nation)
COMMUNIQUÉ, 8 Rue Saint-Sulpice, 6ᵉ (Métro: Saint Sulpice)
LE MOUTON À 5 PATTES, 6 Rue Saint-Sulpice, 6ᵉ (Métro: Sèvres-Babylone)

▼

GIVENCHY: Hubert de Givenchy is the most elegant, handsome man we've ever met, so we forgive him for not making more clothes that we can wear. Shopping his stores is a tad confusing, as there seem to be shops all over

Avenue George V—but it's simple: The couture house is upstairs at 29–31, and only Audrey Hepburn shops there. The men's and women's boutiques are next door to each other, separated by the doorway of another building on the Per Spook side of the street. The men's store is three floors of everything. The women's things are divided into accessories and clothes in two separate shops. Much recent Givenchy ready-to-wear is derivative of Chanel, as is all French *prêt* these days. *Dommage.*

GIVENCHY

3, 8, 29–31 Avenue George V, 8ᵉ (Métro: George V)

66 Avenue Victor Hugo, 16ᵉ (Métro: Victor Hugo)

▼

HERMÈS: We have yearned for the famous Hermès scarf ever since the mid-1960s, when we wished we were old enough, elegant enough, and rich enough to tie one on to the chain links of our handbag straps like everyone else. In those days, an Hermès scarf was a hefty investment at $30. These days the scarves are almost the same price in France and the United States—it hardly pays to travel.

But if you want selection, as in thousands and thousands of choices, be sure to go to the Faubourg shop, the "mother store."

Needless to say, Hermès sells much more than scarves. The saddle department is upstairs at the Faubourg shop; the bath towels and porcelains are to the rear. Check out the enamel bracelets, which are *de rigueur* among the horsey set these days. For the person who has everything, the Hermès apron-and-potholder is $100. There's another Hermès in the Hilton Hotel.

Tip: Don't forget to see if your airline sells Hermès scarves in their on-plane shop; these usually cost about $100 and are less than at Hermès.

If you want used Hermès, try our resale resources. Didier Ludot is the most famous specialist for used Hermès. (See page 123.)

HERMÈS, 24 Rue du faubourg-Saint-Honoré, 8ᵉ (Métro: Concorde)

HERMÈS HILTON HOTEL, 18 Avenue de Suffren, 15ᵉ (Métro: Bir-Hakeim)

▼

KENZO: Yes, Kenzo does have a last name; it's Takada. Yes, Kenzo is a Japanese person—but he is a French designer. The clothes are sold in Galeries Lafayette, as well as all over the world, but we try to do our buying in the Place des Victoires store, which is huge, well stocked, well laid out, fun, and part of the glory that is the Place des Victoires. Prices are high, but if you get a sale period everything in the store will be 30% to 50% off. The men's things (which we think are pretty unisex and have bought for ourselves) are downstairs; go up the huge wooden staircase to the large salon above for women's things, shoes, accessories, and everything else.

KENZO, 3 Place des Victoires, 1ᵉʳ (Métro: Bourse)

▼

HIROKO KOSHINO: The store—and the clothes—are very Japanese but are so chic that they seem very French. Hiroko is one of the three Koshino sisters; the other sisters' clothes are sold at Alma, not far away on the Rue du faubourg-Saint-Honoré. The clean lines of the store and the fastidious elegance of the clothes make this just the kind of place you want to stare at, whether you can wear (or afford) these clothes or not. Many of the knits are very Western and will fit into your wardrobe. $250 and up. Great sales.

HIROKO KOSHINO, 43 Rue du faubourg-Saint-Honoré, 8ᵉ (Métro: Concorde)

▼

LACOSTE: Lacoste is one of those tricky status symbols that you assume will be cheaper in France—after all, it is a French brand. Called *le crocodile* in France, that little alligator has created an international empire and a major brouhaha in counterfeitland. The popular children's clothes were created for the American market and are not made in France. You will not find the colored, striped, single knits, the babywear, or much of the fashion line you are used to in France; nor will you beat $13.99 as a U.S. on-sale price for a typical Lacoste short-sleeve polo shirt.

If you buy in France, you will pay $20–$40 for a short-sleeve shirt! A bathing suit may be $50! Kids' windbreakers are $75 to $100!

BOUTIQUE LACOSTE, 372 Rue Saint-Honoré, 8ᵉ (Métro: Concorde)

▼

LACROIX: You no longer need to be a couture customer to buy a little something from Christian Lacroix, the hottest designer in France (maybe the world) these days. Lacroix was recently selling a *papier-mâché* bracelet in Bergdorf Goodman in New York for $950, so count on the prices being a tad high. Nonetheless, walk in and examine this small space with its carpet and back wall coordinated to a hot raspberry splash of dash and delight. Clothes and accessories are sold—sunglasses with polka dots, handbags, dresses that have flounces and teeth and cost $2,500–$5,800 each. It's very exciting visually.

LACROIX, 73 Rue du faubourg-Saint-Honoré, 8ᵉ (Métro: Miromesnil)

▼

KARL LAGERFELD/REVILLON: Revillon owns Lagerfeld's ready-to-wear line, so the two have teamed up in a new let's-shout-about-it store which is a must-visit for students of architecture and late 1980s chic. Clothes and accessories and fragrance are on the first floor, furs are upstairs. Every aspect of this business is drop-dead chic. Don't miss it.

KARL LAGERFELD/REVILLON, 17 Rue du faubourg-Saint-Honoré, 8ᵉ (Métro: Concorde)

▼

LALIQUE: One glance at Lalique's crystal door and there's no doubt that you've entered one of the wonders of the world. Believe it or not, René Lalique began work as a silversmith, but switched to jewelry-making in 1894. One of his first customers was Sarah Bernhardt, who adored his crystal hair combs, and, as they say in clichés, the rest is history. Today Cristal Lalique is sold in 110 countries. We found the Rue Royale headquarters to have a fabulous selection of everything—including things we didn't know Lalique produced—and a surprising number of things at affordable prices. The prices were the same as at our sources on the Rue de Paradis, by the way, so don't think you may beat the tags here. Besides, you get *détaxe*, and everyone is friendly, speaks English, and ships to the United States.

CRISTAL LALIQUE, 11 Rue Royale, 8ᵉ (Métro: Concorde)

LANCÔME: Lancôme—the cosmetics company —has opened what is very much like a cosmetics boutique with a beauty salon upstairs. They don't sell clothes, but the place is so stylish and hip that this is no ordinary *Institut de Beauté*. You must make the usual purchase to get *détaxe*, which means that unless you are stocking up you may not want to buy here, but this is a gorgeous, gorgeous piece of space. The salon upstairs is very soothing, but they do not offer manicures. Lancôme prices are the same everywhere. Stop by just to gawk if you don't need a massage.

LANCÔME, 29 Rue du faubourg-Saint-Honoré, 8ᵉ (Métro: Concorde)

▼

LANVIN: The House of Lanvin is one of the oldest and best known of French couturiers, due mostly to the successful American advertising campaign for their fragrances My Sin and Arpège (Promise her anything . . .). In recent years, the ready-to-wear (somewhat affordable) line has been designed by the young and gorgeous Maryll Lanvin (former model), who has added a sense of dash to the clothes and made them acceptable for women under sixty-five.

The house seems to be expanding and has opened a gorgeous men's shop on the Rue de Rivoli, close enough to the Louvre that all culture dropouts can end up here in minutes.

Begin your Lanvin women's ready-to-wear research in the Faubourg-Saint-Honoré shop, where the outside of the building is decorated with a giant logo just like a perfume bottle. Before you blow your trust fund (average price in here is $350 per item), remember that other big names cost the same amount of money and may be more your style.

LANVIN, 2 Rue du faubourg-Saint-Honoré, 8ᵉ (Métro: Concorde)

LANVIN SPORT, 2 Rue Cambon, 1ᵉʳ (Métro: Concorde)

LANVIN TAILLEUR, 15 Rue du faubourg-Saint-Honoré, 8ᵉ (Métro: Concorde)

▼

PHILIPPE MODEL: Have you ever looked at those pictures of the fashion showings (couture and *prêt*) in your *WWD* or *W* and fallen in love with the hats that have been teamed with the clothes? If so, you'll be pleased to find Model, who makes many of the hats and who is famous for his inventive and slightly crazy and very stylish *chapeaux.* There are also shoes. This shop happens to be catty-corner to Castelbajac, behind the Hôtel Meurice.

PHILIPPE MODEL, 33 Place du marché Saint-Honoré, 1ᵉʳ (Métro: Pyramides)

▼

THIERRY MUGLER: The little shop on the Place des Victoires will give you the idea. All you have to do is imagine the white piqué dress we saw that was flounced, then starched: that's the look from Mugler—pure and outrageous, both at the same time. The newer shop gives you more of the same but in a selling space that puts a museum to shame—walk down a longish entry after you are inside, and into a salon of selling space. Along the way you'll pass blue lights and modern art and a few spare articles of clothing. Yet the two center areas give you plenty of room to see the clothes. Certainly a look you'll never forget.

THIERRY MUGLER
    49 Avenue Montaigne, 8ᵉ (Métro: Alma)
    Place des Victoires, 2ᵉ (Métro: Bourse)

BERNARD PERRIS: The clothes are architectural and expensive but of good quality and high style. Don't be shy—go look at everything. Even if you don't buy, prowl around and soak up the glamour.

BERNARD PERRIS, 21 Avenue de l'Opéra, 1er (Métro: Opéra)

▼

D. PORTHAULT: Porthault was making fancy bed linens with pretty colored flowers on them long before the real world was ready for patterned sheets or the notion that a person could spend $1,000 on a set of sheets and matching pillowcases and still be able to sleep at night.

There are *two* Porthaults for sale in America: One is identical to what you buy in France, and just costs more in the United States; the other is contracted by the Porthault family and is available only in the United States. Porthault has released one fabric design a year to an American sheet company (both Dan River and Wamsutta have had the honor) for sheets that look but do not feel like their French counterparts. French Porthault is only percale or voile, with some tablecloths done in linen, but with less and less linen being made. There is also no fitted sheet in the French line (you can have one custom-made for extra money).

The French laminated products are not sold in the United States; the American wallpaper is not sold in France. One Porthault saleswoman swore that our pattern was not "theirs" because she was unfamiliar with the American wallpapers. The Montaigne shop does have one whopper of a sale in January during which they unload everything at half the retail price, or less! You cannot phone orders from the United States—we tried.

D. PORTHAULT, 18 Avenue Montaigne, 8e (Métro: Alma Marceau)

NINA RICCI: We're going to tell the truth here, just because it may help you out. Otherwise we'd rather pretend we were more sophisticated. It took us two years to get up the courage to walk into Nina Ricci. Although we passed the building at least ten times a day every time we went to Paris, we never had the nerve to go in. Finally, we did it. It was about 5 P.M. on New Year's Eve, and one of us suddenly decided she had to have something fabulous to go in her hair. Something fabulous like the hair comb the mannequin in the window was wearing. Enter as a serious shopper. We did find the hair comb, with feathers and ribbons and froth—but it cost $660. *But* everyone was so nice that we returned on another occasion. And that's how we found out about the secret room downstairs.

Downstairs is where the samples are sold. There is a large and incredible selection of evening gowns. We saw a black cocktail dress that had chiffon and feathers and sequins and probably a piece of an angel's wing and had been marked down three times to the final resting price of $60. We saw an honest-to-goodness Saudi princess picking out a gown. There are over a hundred gowns here at any given time, as well as a few dresses and suits. Everything downstairs is in size 38.

If you don't need a ball gown but are looking for an impressive gift to give someone you want to impress, consider the Ricci gift department, which is small enough to consider with one big glance. There are $25 gift items here that will be wrapped in Ricci wrap to ensure that they look like a million. Sale gift items will not be wrapped, by the way.

NINA RICCI, 39 Avenue Montaigne, 8ᵉ; closed Saturday, and closed every day from 1 to 2 P.M. (Métro: Alma Marceau)

▼

RODIER: Our favorite Rodier shop in Paris is the Avenue Victor Hugo location (called Rodier Étoile by management), because it is about three times larger than most of the Rodier shops. Rodier makes knits that are ideal for travel, so we follow their designs faithfully. Their big sale is in January; there is another sale in July. A small rack of sale items remains constant through most of the year in the back right-hand corner of the shop—look for an item to fill out some of the pieces you already have or the colors that weren't too popular at all but are at giveaway prices. They also provide a price list to each item in the catalogue so you don't feel embarrassed (or drive them nuts) by asking price after price.

Rodier's corporate offices are at 11 Boulevard de la Madeleine, just a stone's throw from Fauchon. While the empire is run from upstairs, there is a discount shop downstairs where returns, seconds, and out-of-season merchandise are sold. The shop is confusing to find because it appears that a Bally shoe shop is at 11 Boulevard de la Madeleine, so you are tempted to shrug your shoulders and figure, "Ah, lost again." You must enter the driveway at No. 11, hugging the wall to your right so you do not get run over by an approaching car and so you don't miss the door in midarchway that leads to Rodier's offices. The discount shop carries men's and women's things, Rodier and Lacoste. We've never seen anything to get overly excited about. A nice sweater costs $50, but you can get a nice sweater for $50 in many shops in many parts of the world.

RODIER STOCK
11 Boulevard de la Madeleine, 1ᵉʳ (Métro: Madeleine)

RODIER ÉTOILE, 15 Avenue Victor Hugo, 16ᵉ (Métro: Victor Hugo)

RODIER RIVE-GAUCHE, 35 Rue de Sèvres, 6ᵉ (Métro: Sèvres-Babylone)

SONIA RYKIEL: Sonia Rykiel began rewriting fashion history when she was pregnant and couldn't find a thing to wear; her children's line was born when she became a grandmother. She originally knit some fabulous sweaters for herself and word got around—soon she was knitting for others; soon she was famous for her knits worldwide. She's introduced inside-out seams, fanny wraps, and slouch, and continues to pay no heed to the rest of Parisian fashion as she invents and reinvents her own things. While her U.S. line (Sonia Rykiel Knits) has sadly gone out of business, her French clothes are alive and well and as expensive as all get-out.

We have never found a ready supply of Sonia at any of our discount sources. Sonia pops up in neat array at Réciproque—but because a Sonia design can be worn for only so many years, the items there are often well out of style. Rykiel herself encourages hoarding of her clothes and lots of mixing and matching. The department stores have some selection of Sonia, but prices still are high.

SONIA RYKIEL

 4 and 6 Rue de Grenelle, 6ᵉ (Métro: Saint-Sulpice)

 70 Rue du faubourg-Saint-Honoré , 8ᵉ (Métro: Concorde)

SONIA ENFANT, 8 Rue de Grenelle, 6ᵉ (Métro: Saint-Sulpice)

▼

YVES SAINT LAURENT: Rive Gauche shops are going through enormous organizational changes; many U.S. franchises have closed. But Saint Laurent is far from finished.

The newest YSL ready-to-wear line, Variations, is a less expensive YSL creation and is more like a boutique line than a cheapie line. Rive Gauche franchises have the opportunity to buy from the line, but most are doing so on a small scale so as not to lose their high-rolling customers. The full Variations line is difficult to find at any Rive Gauche but is well represented in Galeries Lafayette and many American department stores. You will also find it at Mendès and our favorite resale outlets. The couture remains the ultimate statement of chic and creativity.

RIVE GAUCHE

19–21 Avenue Victor Hugo, 16ᵉ (Métro: Victor Hugo)

38 Rue du faubourg-Saint-Honoré, 8ᵉ (Métro: Concorde)

6 Place Saint-Sulpice, 6ᵉ (Métro: Saint-Sulpice)

12 Rond Point des Champs-Élysées, 8ᵉ (Métro: F. D. Roosevelt)

YSL COUTURE, 43 Avenue Marceau (Métro: Alma Marceau)

▼

JEAN-LOUIS SCHERRER: Scherrer is not young and kicky but classic and elegant. If you love an expensive-looking suit, a fabulous silk two-piece, or the look of an international wheeler and dealer, his clothes are for you. The entire collection, couture and ready-to-wear, is on the Avenue Montaigne; there is an additional boutique on the Rue du faubourg-Saint-Honoré. The elegant stone-fronted Montaigne address is high-tech and elegant all at the same time.

If you love the look but the prices make you wince, there is a shop that sells whatever hasn't moved from the season before. Called the Boutique de Soldes, this shop is so elegant that they hand out those fancy French engraved calling cards! The Boutique de Soldes is not in an especially elegant neighborhood; they have rarely seen an American tourist and speak only spotty English. The great thing about a trip there, however, is that besides the wonderful bargains, you are not far from two other good discount resources, Betty and Rodier.

JEAN-LOUIS SCHERRER
  51 Avenue Montaigne, 8e (Métro: F. D. Roosevelt)
  31 Rue de Tournon, 6e (Métro: Odéon)
SCHERRER BOUTIQUE, 90 Rue du faubourg-Saint-Honoré, 8e (Métro: Concorde)
BOUTIQUE DE SOLDES, 29 Avenue Ledru-Rollin, 12e; hours: 10 A.M. to 6 P.M.; closed Saturday and Sunday; closed Wednesday in April and August (Métro: Ledru-Rollin)

▼

PER SPOOK: The men's and women's shops adjoin, but we go to Per Spook mostly to look at the luggage, which is exactly what we would buy ... if only we needed more luggage. The very large, light, high-tech shop is a showcase for the easily wearable Spook designs, which are pricey for a designer that most Americans have never heard of, but you must remember that this Norwegian shows a couture collection that puts him in the league with the big boys. In couture, the designs are young, fresh, and original. In ready-to-wear, it's much the same as what you get from any hip designer.

PER SPOOK, 18 Avenue George V, 8e (Métro: George V)

▼

ANGELO TARLAZZI: This fabulous *créateur* and design genius has shops on the Left Bank and the Right Bank, where you can marvel at and delight in his talents, whether you can afford them or not. He's a cross between Sonia Rykiel and Perry Ellis, while still being inventive on his own.

Tarlazzi also does a cheapie line called

Tarlazzi II. On sale, a Tarlazzi II dress is about $150.

ANGELO TARLAZZI

67 Rue du faubourg-Saint-Honoré, 8ᵉ (Métro: Miromesnil)

74 Rue des Saints-Pères, 7ᵉ (Métro: Saint-Germain-des-Près)

▼

EMANUEL UNGARO: Translate the color of the rainbow through the eyes of a maven from Provence and you get the palette Ungaro is famous for. When the clothes hang in the Faubourg-Saint-Honoré shop, you can look in the window and see the colors shimmering in the light. The couture house is a series of three chambers that connect on the Rue Montaigne, so you can see many aspects of the line in one larger space. Don't be afraid to walk in, shoulders back, and take a look. There is a back room that often houses sale merchandise—it's straight forward as you enter, but without windows—in the grand salon. Expect to pay $1,000 for a sale garment. Samples from the shows also may be on sale, as well as items used for photographs. We found a necklace lent to *Vogue* on sale for $100—a good buy considering the necklace.

The less expensive line is called Parallèle; an even cheaper line, called Solo Donna, has just been introduced. It's made by GFT and is affordable.

EMANUEL UNGARO

2 Avenue Montaigne, 8ᵉ (Métro: Alma Marceau)

25 Rue du faubourg-Saint-Honoré, 8ᵉ (Métro: Concorde)

▼

VALENTINO: If you are staying at the Plaza Athenée, you have two extra treats to contend with—Chez Francis, the bistro on the corner at Place de l'Alma, and Valentino. The Valentino Piú is gone, so there's more room for men's and women's clothes and more goodies for us to drool over.

You will not find any of the Valentino cheapie lines in this beige marble and glass palace—this is couture only, as fits the address. There is a shop on Rue du faubourg-Saint-Honoré that tells them, however: Maxandre.

VALENTINO, 17–19 Avenue Montaigne, 8ᵉ (Métro: Alma Marceau)

MAXANDRE, 42 Rue du faubourg-Saint-Honoré, 8ᵉ (Métro: Concorde)

▼

LOUIS VUITTON: Louis Vuitton himself opened his first shop in 1854 and didn't become famous for his initials until 1896, when his son came out with a new line of trunks. Things haven't been the same since. The Louis Vuitton shop near the Étoile is nestled off the Arc de Triomphe (around the corner from Le Drugstore) and is a bit hard to find unless you have the street address in your hand. It's not the kind of store you would wander upon while browsing the neighborhood, and if it were not on the same street as one of our favorite bargain basements (Babs, see page 124), we never would have known it existed. Often filled with Japanese tourists, Louis Vuitton is spacious, light-filled, and a minimuseum to the man with the magic initials. The door is guarded by the sternest doorman in Paris, the antique LV pieces that line the entryway are treated as archaeological relics that Indiana Jones might want, and the staff is there to take you by the hand and guide you to a purchase or two or three. You are assigned a salesperson as you walk in and will have trouble being left alone to browse.

In recent years, Vuitton has had so much

trouble with forgeries that they have just rede-
signed their tooling to make a new generation
of fakes all but impossible. There now are
zillions of new LV's dancing around the border in an odd assortment of shapes.

For the real thing but at reduced rates, be
sure to check out our resale resources. We
spied the largest suitcase (La Stratos) in a
resale shop for about $125 last year.

LOUIS VUITTON
   78 bis Avenue Marceau, 8ᵉ (Métro: George V)
   57 Avenue Montaigne, 8ᵉ (Métro: Alma
   Marceau)

Department Stores

French department stores are for French
people; only Galeries Lafayette and Au
Printemps make a serious attempt to woo
American tourists. As a result, Americans
know about these two—which are next door
to each other and easily hit at once—but aren't
very familiar with the other stores, which offer
many of the same services and may be a lot
more fun. Let's get a grip on our definition of
fun. Fun in a Parisian department store is:

▼ hordes of people, especially on weekends and
lunch hours and especially, especially in summer;

▼ merchandise so profuse that often it cannot
even be displayed but merely is dumped in
bins or laid on tables;

▼ many different buildings that are part of the
same store so you can get lost (or found) or
have the pleasure of being in four different
stores before realizing you've never left one;

▼ the ability to see every new trend, fad, and
fashion in one fell swoop; and

▼ the ability to see how the real people of France dress and shop.

If your time in Paris is limited, check out the designer fashions and then all the ready-to-wear clothing floors of a good department store and you will immediately know what's hot and what's not. Spend an hour (maximum, two hours) at Galeries Lafayette's first- and second-floor designer niches for a fast overview of the fashion scene and of what's available. If you have no time to track down the individual shops of your favorite designers, buy at Galeries Lafayette. If you are appalled by the amount of money you now need to spend to get *détaxe*, you can't have a better plan than to shop at a department store, where you can save your receipts and get the *détaxe* on the grand total. Department stores also have help that speaks whatever language you care to speak, and will arrange shipping for you, if need be. Department stores do provide one-stop shopping.

Collector's card. If you are planning on buying a lot, but it will be a lipstick here, some panty hose there, a blouse on two, and a toy on five, and the thought of writing up all those sales slips on an individual basis makes you nuts, you can use a collector's card. Your purchase is rung up on the cash register, held at the desk, and your card is marked with the amount. You go around shopping all day, clutching your card in your hand. When you are finished, you pay for the grand total. This is one of the easiest ways to get your *détaxe*, since you pay and claim the credit all at once. The only problem: After you have paid, you must collect all of your packages. Arrangements may even be made at some stores to ship your purchases directly home.

AU PRINTEMPS: Most people call it merely Printemps, which means spring. Usually we walk in feeling like spring and come out an hour later like a lion in winter. This store has fabulous graphics; they do very nice ads in *The New York Times* inviting you to visit them; often they do promotional tie-ins with tour groups and airlines, and even may offer a 10% discount coupon; they have the very nicest fashion show in the rooftop garden, but still they are a very disappointing store. We have spent years trying to like this store—to little avail. Created in 1865, Au Printemps is based on the Boulevard Haussmann, but has four other branch stores. The main store is divided into three separate stores: Brummel, the men's store, which is behind the main store; the House Store, or Magasin Havre; and the New Store, Nouveau Magasin, women's fashions.

In terms of ambience, Printemps feels a lot like a zoo. The store is the cage and you are trapped. Summer days are murder. Winter is a lot better.

The best things about Au Printemps are simple:

▼ good shoe and lingerie departments
▼ excellent design (home fashion) floors (seven and eight of Magasin Havre)
▼ lovely terrace for seeing Paris
▼ good touristy fashion show (Tuesday all year round at 10 A.M.; also on Friday at 10 A.M. during the high season, March 1 to the end of August)
▼ nice branch stores (there's an especially nice store in Deauville)

AU PRINTEMPS, 64 Boulevard Haussmann, 9e (Métro: Chaussée-d'Antin)
PRINTEMPS TERNES, 30 Avenue des Ternes, 17e (Métro: Ternes)
PRINTEMPS NATION, 25 Cours de Vincennes, 20e (Métro: Porte de Vincennes)
PRINTEMPS ITALIE, 30 Avenue d'Italie, 13e (Métro: Italie)
PRINTEMPS RÉPUBLIQUE, 10 Place de la République, 11e (Métro: République)

AUX TROIS QUARTIERS: If your French is as bad as ours, you'll call this the Three-Quarter Store and be done with it. This is another store that has two parts—the Madelios is the men's store and it's very British, very BCBG. The main store has a very proper tearoom where all the old ladies with blue hair meet to talk about their children. The store is never as crowded as the others, and can offer easy shopping services.

About this store:

▼ It's convenient.

▼ You can see lots of *haute* couture in one swoop.

▼ There's a good toy department.

▼ It's well-known for its hair accessory and hat department.

Hours: 9:30 A.M. to 6:30 P.M.

AUX TROIS QUARTIERS, 17 Boulevard de la Madeleine, 1ᵉʳ (Métro: Madeleine)

▼

BAZAR DE L'HÔTEL DE VILLE: If you think that's a funny name for a store, you can call it BHV (pronounced Bay H. Vay in French), or remember that the name of the store tells you just where it is—directly across from the Hôtel de Ville, or City Hall of Paris.

The store is famous for its do-it-yourself attitude and for its housewares, although you probably aren't shopping for housewares while in Paris. We wish we could tell you that BHV was better organized than the other department stores, but we would be sent to our rooms without dinner and our noses would grow long.

Pointers on BHV:

▼ It's not so much like a U.S. department store as a dime store, even though they do carry Rodier and some big names.

▼ The tearoom and rest rooms are worth forgetting.

▼ There's a great outdoor *crêpe* stand half a block away as you get out of the *métro*.

▼ It has a good souvenir department.

▼ There's an amazing do-it-yourself department.

▼ It's incredible for pots and pans; cooks will go wild!

Hours: Monday, Tuesday, Thursday, Friday, and Saturday, 9:30 A.M. to 6:30 P.M.; Wednesday, 9:30 A.M. to 10 P.M.

BHV, Rue de Rivoli, 1er (Métro: Hôtel-de-Ville)

▼

BON MARCHÉ: Bon Marché is the big department store of the Left Bank. While there are branches of some of the other stores on the Left Bank, this is the one biggie there, and it is convenient to a good bit of your Left Bank shopping. Bon Marché looks a bit like Harrods in the grand old-fashioned department store tradition, and is rumored to be the secret inspiration for Henri Bendel's street of shops. There are two stores, actually, but the smaller one is devoted to food and entertaining and connects through the basement to the main store. We've found some fun here because the first floor really seems to have a well-chosen little bit of everything. The food part is marvelous—all the housewives are here to buy the makings of their dinner parties because the prices are less than at LeNotre but the quality is almost as good. This is the Bloomie's of the Left Bank.

Hours: Monday to Saturday, 9:30 A.M. to 6:30 P.M.

BON MARCHÉ, Rue de Sèvres, 6e (Métro: Sèvres-Babylone)

▼

C&A: This is a Dutch department store famous for its low-end merchandise, rather like Marks & Spencer. You'll find them all over the world. The clothes have more zip to them than at Marks & Spencer; often you can find cute copies of the fad fashions at prices that are appropriate for teens. C&A in Paris is convenient, inexpensive, manageable, and even has nice dressing rooms.

Hours: Monday to Saturday, 9:30 A.M. to 7 P.M.

C&A

124 Rue de Rivoli, 1er (Métro: Châtelet)

22 Rue du Depart, 14e (Métro: Montparnasse)

▼

FRANCK ET FILS: Franck et Fils actually is a specialty store. Grandma Sara used to shop at the Blum Store in Philadelphia, and that is precisely what Franck et Fils is—the kind of place where your rich grandmother buys her silk dresses, gloves, and handkerchiefs. We're talking refined old lady here. Back behind the elevator, there is a telephone that links up directly to a taxi company. The store is elegant, easy to shop, not crowded, and remains unknown to tourists. The Chanel jewelry selection is excellent.

Hours: Monday to Saturday, 10 A.M. to 5:30 P.M.

FRANCK ET FILS, 80 Rue de Passy, 16e (Métro: Muette)

▼

GALERIES LAFAYETTE: Galeries Lafayette loves tourists and very much wants you to spend your money with them. Since a hundred thousand people a day (!!!) visit this store, they obviously have convinced a lot of customers. Whenever we go to Galeries Lafayette we remember the expression "Hell is other people." Well, hell is other people who shop at

Galeries Lafayette. Especially in summer. If you are strong, then you deserve to see the three Galeries Lafayette stores: Galfa Club (a men's store); the Main Store; and the Sports Store.

There also is a snack shop and restaurant called Pavillon Lafayette, 14 Rue de Mogador, 9ᵉ, behind the main store.

We think Galeries Lafayette is a better store than Printemps, if you are trying to choose between them. Usually we spend some time in both, since they are next to each other.

Hours: 9:30 A.M. to 6:30 P.M.; closed Sunday.

GALERIES LAFAYETTE, 40 Boulevard Haussmann, 9ᵉ (Métro: Chaussée-d'Antin)
GALERIES LAFAYETTE CENTRE COMMERCIAL MONTPARNASSE, 22 Rue du Départ, 14ᵉ (Métro: Montparnasse)

▼

MARKS & SPENCER: On Boulevard Haussmann you can zigzag into the Opéra or go immediately into Marks & Spencer. Which would you rather, really? The Marks & Spencer in Paris is amazingly like the main one near Selfridge's in London. Marks & Spencer still is a good place for underwear, for the St. Michael private brand, and for good, sturdy, inexpensive kids' clothes. But it is a far from elite store, and blue bloods should pass without entering.

Hours: Monday, Tuesday, Thursday, Friday, and Saturday, 9:30 A.M. to 6:30 P.M.; Wednesday, 10 A.M. to 6:30 P.M.

MARKS & SPENCER, 33–45 Boulevard Haussmann, 9ᵉ (Métro: Chaussée-d'Antin)

▼

SAMARITANE: We've heard complaints about Samaritane, since it's so confusing with

the separate stores and the interconnecting basement, but we really like this store better than
most and we encourage you to have fun here.
It is very French. They probably haven't seen
an American since we left. To explain why: Of
the four buildings that make up the store, only
one of them is even called Samaritane. The
most important shop is Store 2, which is behind Store 4 and isn't directly on the Rue de
Rivoli.

The sports department is in Store 3. Store 1
is partially open. Store 4 has records and books
and art supplies and is a favorite stop of ours.
But Store 2 is what you want; it also is the
only one with a bathroom.

About Samaritane:

▼ We never buy anything here, we just look.
▼ If you want designer clothes, this is not
the place to look.
▼ The food selection is good.
▼ The view from the roof garden is fabulous.

Hours: Monday, Wednesday, Thursday, and
Saturday, 9:30 A.M. to 7 P.M.; Tuesday and
Friday, 9:30 A.M. to 8:30 P.M.

SAMARITANE, 67 Rue de Rivoli, 1ᵉʳ (Métro:
Châtelet)

Shopping Centers

The shopping centers of your teen years,
like the mall where everyone used to
hang out, do not exist in great abun-
dance in Europe. The Forum des Halles
was built to rejuvenate a slum, and serves as
an exciting monument to youth, style, and
shopping. We adore the entire Les Halles area
all the way to the Pompidou. (This area around

the Centre Georges Pompidou is called the Beaubourg.) All the young, kicky designers and retailers are here—you can browse and/or buy to your heart's content. You'll find inexpensive restaurants, walk-in hair salons, discounters, and designers surrounding the actual Forum as well as in the Forum itself.

The Forum des Halles is a three-story square complex that rises above part of a *métro* station (Châtelet). There are fast-food joints in the *métro* part of the complex and real restaurants in among the shops in the regular complex. A series of escalators zigzags the floors; there are master maps with little lights on them so you can find where you want to go. The Forum was built in stages, so be sure to see the newest part of the mall, which stretches underground.

Most of the stores in the Forum des Halles open from 10 to 10:30 A.M. and close at 7 to 7:30 P.M., and are closed all day Sunday and Monday morning (but open at noon on Monday). All take plastic.

There also are several indoor groups of stores that may be called a shopping center, or a big *passage*, on the Champs-Élysées. The Champs-Élysées became a really hot address for a shop after World War II, and to create space in the office buildings that line the boulevard from Rond Point on up, the lobby space was filled with shopping arcades. Most are very glitzy; several have intricate water fountains in the center. See our section on the Champs-Élysées for the blow-by-blow.

In this same style but more like an American mall is the space in the even more modern Montparnasse Commercial Center complex. These stores actually are for the business community that works in this tower, and we feel very strongly that tourists have other stores to conquer before they race over here.

Passages

No offense to Gail Sheehy, but in France a *passage* is not a "Passage." A *passage* (it rhymes with massage) is a shopping area, exactly like an arcade in London. *Passages* are the equivalent of minimalls, and are cut into a building's lobby like a throughway. In the early 1800s the buildings were large, often taking up a block. To get from one side to the other at midpoint, a *passage* was built. It is inside the building, so it's totally covered. Doorways lead through the original structure.

There are zillions of *passages* all over Paris. One of the most famous *passages* is the Galerie Vivienne, which is more of a freestanding *passage* than others. One doorway is on the Rue Vivienne, the other is on the Rue des Petits-Champs. The *passage* is not surrounded by a greater building but is directly across from the National Library and near the Palais-Royal.

The shopowners in a *passage* usually organize themselves, at least informally. Together they will decide if their shops will be open or closed during lunchtime. (The Galerie Vivienne is open during lunchtime.) *Passages* have cheaper rent than regular commercial space, so usually you'll find relatively mundane enterprises (like a printer or bakery) or young designers who are just starting out but may be moving fast.

Métro Shopping

Most of the *métro* stops have little shops in them. These are the kind of shops you find in almost any *métro* or subway—overpriced and not of good quality. The Châtelet station is gigantic (many lines converge here) and so has more of an underground shopping mall built into it than do other stops. You always can buy postcards and souvenirs in these shops. Often street people set up their wares on blankets in the stations. You can bargain here, of course, but watch for fakes. *Métro* stop souvenirs are inexpensive and make unique gifts.

The Duty-frees

We wish we could give you the last word on duty-free shops. Instead we find ourselves in a love-hate relationship. For the most part we have always thought that duty-free shops were a gimmick. They trick you into believing that they offer less expensive prices with the misleading term "duty-free" and then have a few bargain items and lots of expensive items—but you are too confused to know the difference. On the other hand, for certain types of merchandise, a duty-free is heaven.

There are duty-free shops in town and at the airport; their prices are all the same. In fact, on standard items (cosmetics and booze), all duty-frees in a specific community offer the same prices, because these are set by law. A duty-free shop is a discounter, selling at a 20%

discount merchandise that suppliers allow to be sold at discount. La Prairie does not release its products to duty-free shops. Lancôme does a huge business with duty-frees. Some American cosmetics companies sell goods at duty-frees; mostly the prices are outrageous: $5 for a bottle of Revlon nail polish.

Duty-free shops are a good place to buy fragrances and cosmetics, although the price on these items is controlled and may offer you little or no savings. This is why we give you the speech about doing your homework. Saving $1 on a Lancôme mascara is not our idea of anything to brag about. Sometimes the savings are related to the cost of the dollar. When the dollar was high, we saved $4 on a Lancôme mascara. Now the dollar is lower, and Lancôme prices are higher. Life goes on. Chanel lipstick, which is $14 in the United States and $10 in Hong Kong, is $8 in Paris. Now, that's a bargain!

By French law, the amount of savings on perfume and toilet water differs. A good duty-free will write your order all as one and give you the maximum discount (sneaky, sneaky). Also by law, the duty-free can give you no more than a 20% discount. You get this discount on one tube of lipstick or on $2,000 worth of merchandise. No more, no less. If, however, you qualify for the *détaxe*, you will get an additional 20% discount. Although one thing has nothing to do with another, duty-frees like to tell you that they give a 40% discount to make you feel like a lucky duck. To get the 40% discount, *you must qualify for the détaxe*. On the other hand, if you want just a few items and can't begin to think about spending nearly $200, it makes the most sense to shop at a duty-free rather than any other type of makeup store, including a large department store—*except* if you are saving your department store receipts to qualify for the *détaxe* (see pages 37 and 108), you can make small makeup purchases. You will not get the 20%

duty-free discount, but you will eventually qualify for the 20% *détaxe* discount. This takes amazing planning.

Most duty-free shops sell makeup, fragrance, and other touristy items with the service policy of being a one-stop shopping resource. This more easily enables you to make the quota for the *détaxe*. So you buy scarves, handbags, hair combs, and other gift items in the free-wheeling belief that you are getting a 40% discount on everything. Wrong. Ask what the discount is on each item you are buying.

Museum Shops

lmost all the Paris museums have gift shops. Some just sell slides, prints, and a few high-minded books. But several are really with it and must have made a trip to the New York Metropolitan Museum of Art to see how it's done. All the fashiony museums have excellent gift shops:

MUSÉE DES ARTS DÉCORATIFS: 107 Rue de Rivoli, 1er (Métro: Louvre). It's closed Mondays and Tuesdays and open on Sundays from 11 A.M. to 5 P.M. The shop and the separate bookstore are wonderful.

MUSÉE DU LOUVRE: Palais du Louvre, 1er (Métro: Louvre). Yes, they do have a gift shop. This is where we bought all those prints to decorate our dorm rooms all those years ago. We just bought a *Mona Lisa* for the Coleytown Elementary School second grade class: 13 francs (less than $3.00).

MUSÉE D'ORSAY: Gare d'Orsay, 7e (Métro: Orsay). The gift shop isn't as wonderful as the architecture, but you can buy prints and some reproductions and a scarf or two. Good selection of postcards.

CENTRE GEORGES POMPIDOU: Centre Georges Pompidou, 4ᵉ (Métro: Châtelet). The gift shop takes up much of the first floor and is a wonderful source for posters and books and postcards. They have the special tubes you need to transport posters so they don't get crushed.

Souvenir Shops

P aris is loaded with souvenir shops. They congregate around the obvious tourist haunts (Notre Dame, Champs-Élysées, etc.) and line the Rue de Rivoli from Concorde all the way up to the front gate of the Louvre. They all sell more or less the same junk at exactly the same prices. Yes, folks, the prices are fixed. The only way you can get a break on the price is to deal on the amount you buy. When we were planning on buying one hundred bath-sponge replicas of the Eiffel Tower, we were able to negotiate a price break—if we paid in cash. If you buy a few T-shirts, you might get a few francs knocked off the price.

Special-Event Retailing

O ne of our favorite shopping events is the Braderie de Paris, which is held in December and June at the Porte de Versailles. It's rather like a church bazaar. Speaking French will help but is not required.

All the big designers donate items for sale; there are bargains by the ton. Ask your concierge for details and the exact dates, although the event will be advertised in magazines and papers, and we know you read *Madame Figaro* when you are in town, so you probably know it all anyway. There is easy access by *métro*.

Hermès has sales twice a year that can only be described as a world-class sporting event. Held in March and October, the sales' exact dates are revealed moments before, in ads in the newspapers. Lines begin to form at 7 A.M.; a lucky few are let in when the doors open at 10 A.M. The average wait in line is four hours before admission; items are marked down to just about half price. Lest you gloat too long over the bargain, there is a code worked into your purchase that tells the world your item was bought on sale. It is not obvious, but look for a teeny-tiny S in the scarf, etc.

The thing you really want to catch is the Biennale Internationale des Antiquaires, which is an international antiques fair. We are not talking small-time international antiques fair with a few dozen chairs and a sofa half eaten by moths. This is the single biggest, most important antiques event in the world. Usually it is held in September and is at the Grand Palais—which is midpoint between the Place de la Concorde and Rond Point and is most easily reached by a *métro* that comes up right next to it.

The big catch is that the major show is every other year. Check in the design trades for the actual dates, ask your decorator, or check with your concierge. You need not be a designer to attend.

Annual shows are held at the Grand Palais each end of November through early December, and they, too, are wonderful, but if you've ever been to the big event, you surely will never forget it.

The French tourist office also can supply you with the dates of these special events and others—antiques shows and special sales, conventions, trade shows, and whatnot. Write to the French Government Tourist Office, 610 Fifth Avenue, New York, NY 10020-2493.

Dépôts-Ventes (Resale Shops)

RÉCIPROQUE: These are actually three separate shops in a row. The main Réciproque shop has two floors, so don't forget to go downstairs. There are racks and racks of clothes, all clean—there're separates, shoes, evening clothes, and complete ensembles. You must look through carefully and know your merchandise, although the labels always are in the clothes. Not everything is used, or seriously used—many designers sell samples or photography items. Every big name is represented here; this is the best single resource for ladies who wear couture to sell their used clothes.

In the gift shop we found good buys in silver, tablecloths, and china. This is obviously a hit-or-miss operation, but give it a look-see. We saw the world's most stunning sterling silver service for $2,500. Back to earth, a Richard Ginori tea and coffee pot set was $50. You also can buy used sports equipment (downstairs from gifts), children's clothes, and jewels.

RÉCIPROQUE, 95 Rue de la Pompe, 16ᵉ (Métro: Pompe)

▼

ELLIPSE: While Caméléon (see following listing) has the feel of a resale shop, Ellipse feels like a small but fashionable boutique. They have new merchandise scattered with the used—there were two brand-new, current-season Hermès handbags at half their Faubourg price. They do not speak much English, but the shop is very nice and you are treated like a real lady. If you buy a lot, ask about a 10% discount. You can also ask about *détaxe*, but we've never found a resale shop that will give it to us. (You can start by asking for *détaxe*, and when they say no, ask for a smaller discount.) Ellipse is closed Monday.

ELLIPSE, 26 Rue Gustave Courbet, 16ᵉ (Métro: Victor Hugo)

▼

CAMÉLÉON: We once sent a friend to our resale shops and she came away with a complete set of Louis Vuitton luggage—two pieces from Caméléon and one piece from Réciproque. Total cost for all three pieces: $375! This small shop has bins for sweaters, a shoe rack, and several pipe racks, in front and back, for clothes. There are some fur coats. You'll see the usual names you love to see—Yves Saint Laurent, Claude Montana, Ungaro, Sonia, etc. There was some new YSL, with the same pieces in several sizes (this was Rive Gauche YSL). Caméléon is closed Monday.

CAMÉLÉON, 13 Rue Gustave Courbet, 16ᵉ (Métro: Victor Hugo)

▼

DIDIER LUDOT: This shop is not easy to find, so have patience and remember that it is on the gallery side of the building, not the street side. It is a very tiny shop run by a man who really cares about the clothes and their history, and he tries to sell only top-of-the-line used designer goods, specializing in Hermès, Céline, and Chanel. You may find old Hermès bags from the 1930s here. The entire gallery is fun but this store is a standout for old-clothes junkies. Prices are high for quality items.

DIDIER LUDOT, 24 Passage de la Galerie Montpensier, near Palais-Royal, 1er (Métro: Palais-Royal)

Bargain Basements

ANNA LOWE: Since the front of Anna Lowe has her name on the door and then the words *haute couture*, you might think we've made a mistake sending you to such a fancy place. Trust us. Despite the beige marble and the fine windows, Anna Lowe's prices are very low for designs by major names. Prices are not cheap, but these aren't cheap clothes. Prices are at least 25% less than in the Paris shops. This is the kind of shop Mother would call "a good find." They take plastic and speak English. Some of the clothes are models' samples; if you're size 6 or 8 you will do very well here. Hours: Monday to Friday, 10 A.M. to 7 P.M.; note the strange Saturday hours: 3 P.M. to 7 P.M.

ANNA LOWE, 35 Avenue Matignon, 8e (Métro: F. D. Roosevelt)

▼

BABS: The beige carpet and fancy surroundings make it seem unbelievable that this is a bargain basement. The help is not really friendly if you are just browsing, but once you show them you are a serious shopper, things warm up. There always has been an incredible selection of daytime dresses, separates, and evening wear. We found a YSL shirt we had seen at Mendès for $99 at Babs for $49. Ho hum. That doesn't mean Babs always is cheaper; it's just another one of those sad stories. We always ask the help to tell us whose clothes were whose, since many labels are cut out.

BABS, 29 Avenue Marceau, 16ᵉ (Métro: Alma Marceau)

▼

BETTY: After Babs, it's a long way to Betty—on the *métro* and emotionally. But our friend Yvette got the name from a great bargain huntress she met in China, and we thought those credentials made it worth checking out. The bad news about Betty: We don't really think it's our kind of place. The good news about Betty: The shop is across from the *marché* at Place d'Aligre, which is one of the most colorful *marchés* in Paris and is so worth visiting that while you're there, you can stick your head into Betty and check it out. Betty seems to specialize in a lot of whatever she got her hands on. Last year we were there when the Léonard shipment came in. For $250 you could own a current, silk-knot Léonard dress that we don't need to tell you was the bargain of the century. You could get lucky.

Hours: Tuesday, Wednesday, and Friday, 8:30 A.M. to 12:30 P.M.; Thursday and Saturday, 8:30 A.M. to 12:30 P.M. and 2:30 P.M. to 4:30 P.M.

BETTY, 10 Place d'Aligre, 12ᵉ (Métro: Ledru-Rollin)

▼

BERNARD MARIONNAUD: While it is on Avenue Victor Hugo, do not think it's on the Avenue Victor Hugo near the Étoile. This Victor Hugo is in Clamart, which is about five minutes outside of Paris past the Porte de Versailles and is a working-class neighborhood. There are three other outlets of this shop, but they aren't convenient and they don't begin to compare, so we are not telling you where they are. We suggest that you not let anyone talk you into visiting them. But if you are ready for one of the shopping adventures of your life, make the trek out to Clamart.

Bernard Marionnaud is famous in French retailing and perfume circles, because he began the entire discount perfume business. He sells more than fragrance in Clamart, but he is primarily a resource for cosmetics and fragrances. Before we go into rhapsodic rantings and ravings about this store, we offer a warning: You will not get any better price on cosmetics or fragrance here than in Paris. In fact, you may not get the very lowest price on the noncosmetic items, either—but you will get a good low price and will have a great time. What Clamart offers is selection. We have never in our lives seen such a selection, especially at a discount resource. Clamart offers three types of merchandise—regular drugstore sundries (hair spray, curlers, panty hose), designer accessories (S. T. Dupont, Cartier, Balenciaga), and the full line of the world's most famous cosmetics and fragrance companies. Not only do they have every size of perfume and toilet water, but they also have all the promotional gifts—those tote bags filled with sunscreen, the men's dop kit with grooming aids, etc. They even carry Guerlain, which is rather extraordinary, since Guerlain traditionally is sold only in Guerlain shops.

They take credit cards and are extremely friendly. If you don't want to spring for a taxi for the considerable distance, take the *métro* to Porte de Versailles and get a taxi there. Remember that you may not save back your taxi fares, but you will have the time of your life.

Hours: Sunday, 9:30 A.M. to 1 P.M.; Monday, 2 P.M. to 8 P.M.; Tuesday to Saturday, 8:30 A.M. to 8 P.M.

BERNARD MARIONNAUD, 91 Avenue Victor Hugo, Clamart, 16ᵉ (Métro: Porte de Versailles, then taxi)

CHIFF-TIR: Chiff-Tir is not one of the great finds of the Western world—but you probably will walk right by it anyway, so you can decide rather easily if it's your cup of tea. Chiff-Tir is an outlet for linens and tableware. Most French people shop here, especially for their kids' sheets—of which they have a wide selection of the cartoon characters. The sheets happen to be much cheaper than in the United States. If you have a good eye and don't mind looking through some very average merchandise, you can find some nice gifts—or personal items at extremely inexpensive prices. If you entertain outdoors, or have kids, and like your tables to look divine without going the Souleiado-Porthault-Pratesi route, Chiff-Tir may solve your problems.

CHIFF-TIR
134 Rue de Rivoli, 1ᵉʳ (Métro: Louvre)
56 Rue de Seine, 6ᵉ (Métro: Odéon)

▼

L'ANNEXE DES CRÉATEURS: Located on a small street with lots of tiny shops, the Annexe isn't far from Fauchon and the Madeleine.

The shop is crowded, and lacks charm, but is crammed with clothes and bolts of fabric—if you like this kind of thing, we suggest poking your head in. Keep in mind that the location is close to many places in every woman's journey through Paris, so it's no trouble to get there. The store in the 16ᵉ has recently beefed up the stock and is very much worth visiting if you are a steady Loehmann's-type customer who understands the rules of the game.

L'ANNEXE DES CRÉATEURS
19 Rue Godot-de-Mauroy, 9ᵉ (Métro: Madeleine)
11 Rue Bois le Vent, 16ᵉ (Métro: Muette)

▼

LE JARDIN DES SOLDES: This is one of many off-price shops in a string of such. It happens to be across the street from the Porte de Versailles. We like to *métro* here, taxi to Clamart, and then taxi back, do our shopping in these two blocks, and then *métro* back into the city. The shop looks and feels like a shop, and the merchandise is clean and neat. The selection varies; we've found a good bit of New Man there (few labels) and a lot of Italian sweaters that were of good quality but no particular design house we could identify. There's also good-quality children's sportswear.

Hours: Sunday to Friday, 10 A.M. to 7 P.M.; Saturday, 10 A.M. to 12:30 P.M.

LE JARDIN DES SOLDES, 17 bis Boulevard Victor Hugo, 15ᵉ (Métro: Porte de Versailles)

▼

MENDÈS: If you happen to visit Mendès during the summer months you will believe that every American in Paris has come, too. We were there once in July and discovered the only people speaking French were the two salesgirls. We've been going for several years now, at various times of the year, and find it very spotty. February is the best month. Many times we have walked away empty-handed and depressed.

Mendès is a jobber who now owns the rights to Yves Saint Laurent's Rive Gauche. The shop is devoted to various YSL lines, but we have also seen some Lanvin clothes here. There is an upstairs and a ground floor, so see both.

Just because this shop is on Rue Montmartre, do not think it is in the famous section of Paris called Montmartre. It's not. It is about three blocks from the Forum des Halles; just stay on the Rue Montmartre until you get there. The numbers should go down if you're going in the right direction. If you end up on the Rue du faubourg Montmartre, you went the wrong way. (We've done that, too.)

Hours: Monday to Thursday, 9:30 A.M. to 6:30 P.M.; Friday, 9:30 A.M. to 5 P.M.; Saturday, 9:30 A.M. to 4:30 P.M.

MENDÈS, 65 Rue Montmartre, 9ᵉ (Métro: Sentier)

▼

MI-PRIX: This store is far from fancy, if you get our drift. But the bargains—ooh la-la. Mi-Prix has a very weird combination of items—the junkiest of no-name merchandise, some very nice skiwear, a fabulous collection of Maud Frizon and Walter Steiger shoes (and boots), and almost giveaway prices. We are not talking about a few shoes from last year's collection. We're talking a virtual museum to Maud Frizon. The shoes are as current as last season and as old as your grandmother. But Maud is so offbeat that an old pair of shoes can look perfect many years later. And everything is brand new. This is where we got the new Bottega Veneta shoes for $50.

MI-PRIX, 27 Boulevard Victor, 15ᵉ (Métro: Porte de Versailles)

▼

STEPHANE: This is one of our favorite places, mostly because of its aggressive advertising program that makes all the world know that discounting has come to Paris and won't be stopped. If you're a big American football-player type, forget it—little here will fit you. If you are average to small, you may hit the big time with Stephane. Labels are cut out of some garments. Big names are here; some women's suits.

STEPHANE, 5 Rue Washington, 8ᵉ (Métro: George V)

TEXAFFAIRES: Conveniently located between the Forum and the Pompidou, Texaffaires is the outlet for Descamps sheets, towels, and robes. The colors are beautiful, the stock is huge, the light pours through the large windows and makes you want to buy everything in sight, everything in those yummy Descamps colors, anyway. A child's bathrobe is $25; a man's, $50. There's more merchandise downstairs. This is not current stuff, but a terry robe of high quality is a classic—so who cares? Texaffaires is closed Sunday and Monday.

TEXAFFAIRES, 5 Rue Saint Martin, 4ᵉ (Métro: Châtelet)

▼

CHARLES REBB: It's called *discount haute de gamme pour hommes*, and we were game for this shop once we discovered it. It's not far from the Opéra. And if you'll let us get a little lyrical here, just as Opéra is perfection to some buffs, so Rebb is perfection to those men who want style and good prices. This truly is a chic shop as well as a discounter with big-name designer clothes—Ted Lapidus, Daniel Hechter. There're lots of shirts, English traditional looks, and gorgeous shoes—all name brands. This is a real find for men, or for women who like men's sweaters and a unisex look. Prices are excellent, supplies are good. Come and get it.

CHARLES REBB, 24 Rue du 4 Septembre, 2ᵉ (Métro: 4 Septembre)

▼

STOCK BIDERMAN: Located in the République discount area, Biderman is the kind of place where you may buy a quality man's suit at a quality price. Men who always have wanted

Saint Laurent but couldn't afford it may be impressed—and lucky. A true find.

STOCK BIDERMAN, 114 Rue de Turenne, 3ᵉ (Métro: Saint Paul)

▼

LE CLEF DES SOLDES: The business card has an orange key on it, and anyplace that calls itself the key to sales is fine with us. All sorts of clothes are sold here—many are designer things at amazingly low prices. But it is the underwear that makes this a shop never to be forgotten. Weird hours—the store opens every day at 9:45 A.M. and closes at 2:15 P.M. and then reopens at 3:15 P.M. after lunch, until 6 P.M. It's closed all day Sunday and on Monday morning.

LE CLEF DES SOLDES, 99 Rue Saint-Dominique, 7ᵉ (Métro: Ecole Militaire)

7▾ PARIS RESOURCES

The French Couture

While French dressing certainly did not begin on a salad, the couture is considered the epitome of French style. It also has become the international statement of fashion and elegance. *Haute couture* actually means fancy seams, and when you think couture and understand that you are talking about $30,000 garments, you'd better believe that you get very fancy seams.

French couture actually was begun by an Englishman, Charles Frederick Worth, who designed for the Empress Eugénie and created his own distinctive look—flounced skirts balanced by crinolines. (The House of Worth still is known today for its fragrance division, by the way.) Worth worked in the mid- to late 1800s; a new set of couturiers sprang to fame in the turn-of-the-century high-fashion years that ended with World War I. The War to End All Wars also ended a certain life-style forever, and gave much more freedom to women—their garments reflected their change of status, and couturiers such as Paul Poiret and Madeleine Vionnet sprang into vogue for their outlandish designs that had the chutzpah to show off a woman's body.

Christian Dior sparked the world of couture in 1947, right after World War II, with his New Look, and couture has continued to evolve since then as a combination of high style and high inspiration that influenced all other levels of ready-to-wear. Copies of couture designs were first absorbed into the American culture (the Lord & Taylor couture buyer even had to bring her clothes out of Paris through enemy lines during World War I) and made up American fashion until the early 1950s, when the first American designers of ready-to-wear began to emerge. Dior's assistant, Yves Saint Laurent, emerged as the *Wunderkind* of couture in 1959, and a group of Young Turks who today hold the silken threads emerged as the powers that be during this time.

Yet surprisingly, the couture is not made up just of the names you have come to recognize—from the older, well-established names such as Christian Dior (now designed by Marc Bohan) and Hubert Givenchy to the younger names such as Emanuel Ungaro and Yves Saint Laurent. There are many couturiers you have never heard of—they are registered with the Chambre Syndicale de la Couture Parisienne (founded in 1868, my dear) and must meet stringent requirements to be couturiers. They, too, show and do custom work, and every now and then they get discovered by the press and made into stars.

To be accredited by the Chambre, you must:

▼ present a formal, written request to be considered;

▼ establish workrooms in Paris;

▼ present two collections a year, in January and July;

▼ create each collection with seventy-five or more original designs;

▼ employ three models full-time;

▼ employ twenty production workers full-time; and

▼ produce made-to-measure garments, as opposed to ready-to-wear.

Occasionally the head of a house never actually gets the Chambre's approval, so that technically they are not members—such as the House of Balenciaga or Chanel—but when you have that kind of talent, no one seems to remember or care if you are registered.

Although we have just listed the really famous houses in this section, there are many others (about fifty), and there are new ones that come to the fore. Lecoanet-Hemant is still needing press (this is a team, Didier Lecoanet and Hemant Sagar), while Marcel Blanc is using the old-fashioned couture methods to create new-wave clothes—a rather amusing thought. Rock stars love it.

Usually the designer owns the house that bears his name, although in these days of buyouts and takeovers, it is not unusual for a corporation to buy a design firm. The designer makes his name but not his fortune in couture. It costs between $500,000 and $1 million to mount a couture collection these days, and the cost of the clothes does not compensate for the cost of producing them. Yves Saint Laurent considers his couture collection a gift to his customers. Indeed, even at $7,000 to $8,000 for a dress or $10,000 to $20,000 for a suit or gown, the prices are not justified against the man-hours and labor-intensive care that go into this kind of dressmaking.

Who pays that kind of money for a garment? Only a handful of women; there are thought to be less than 2,500 couture customers left in the world. Designers often list the number of regular couture customers they can count. Dior claims about 500 customers; Saint Laurent, some 750. Nonetheless, the opening of a collection is a big event to society ladies, buyers, designers, and the press. While couture showings are held over a period of months and anyone can attend them free, the cachet is in attending the opening, which actually is a press opening. This event is free to press and Ladies (that's with a capital L) who get invitations but costs a *caution* to buyers, which is a fee ranging from $300 to $5,000 per house. The *caution* may be a minimum purchase. The cost of a garment varies and most garments have three prices—the price to a buyer (the steepest); the regular price (about 30% less expensive than the buyer's price); and the sample price, which is the price for the garment shown on the runway and not bespoke, as all other couture garments are. Some buyers pay for the rights to copy the garments they buy; some buy "tissues," which are actual patterns to a style. Pattern companies choose certain tissues and pay for them and then provide a royalty on the pattern. (The Vogue Pattern Company always has provided couture designs to the American sewing public.)

The customer who attends an opening is provided with a pad, a pencil, and a list of the garments to be shown that is much like a menu. Each garment is numbered. The patron either marks the menu by putting an *x* on the style number or marks her pad with the styles she is serious about. Later she will return to the salon and work privately with her own saleswoman or *vendeuse*, who will show her the garments she is interested in. After the selection has been made, Madame will be measured thoroughly. If she is a new customer (Where has Madame been?), a dummy must be built to her exact measurements. If she is a repeat customer, her new measurements will be compared to those of her existing mannequin. There will be three fittings several weeks apart. Every aspect of the garment will be made to measure by hand with exacting care.

You need not be a couture customer to see a collection (thank God). After the big brouhaha has died down at the time of the opening, you are welcome to visit the salon and see the show. You can call a house directly and reserve a seat (seats must be reserved; drop-ins are frowned upon), or ask your hotel concierge to do so. Most tourists rely on the concierge route; you'll show more individual style if you do it yourself. All houses have English-speaking help. Expect to see a videotape after the first few weeks of live previews.

Do not show up in your London Fog raincoat with your camera in hand. If you have a garment made by the designer, it is a nice touch to wear it. You need not. Remember that you will be treated according to how well dressed you are. If possible, arrange to attend the show with someone who buys—you will then be treated with more warmth, and possibly a little respect. Serious customers are known throughout the small world of couture; new customers are introduced to the refined inner workings of the system by their refined (and rich) friends.

But we don't mean to scare you off! You can go to a couture show without the obligation to buy, and you needn't feel shabby just because you haven't got the latest little creation by Karl Lagerfeld dripping from your padded shoulders. Have your self-confidence fully in place. You will not fool the *vendeuse* when you walk into a couture showroom—her trained eye will size up your pocketbook (inside and out) in a matter of seconds. Try for an honest approach like, "I've heard that the couturiers sell their samples at the end of the season. Will you be selling samples here?" Do not ask:

"What size are the samples?" (six)
"Can I afford them?" (If you have to ask . . .)
"Do you take plastic?" (*mais oui*)

A few tips for *les américaines* who make it to the early shows:

▼ Yes, you can wear a hat and gloves and your fur and all your jewelry.

▼ Press shows may or may not be held in the couture house—sometimes they are held in hotels or museums.

▼ The lights will stay on during the show—all the better to see you, my dear.

▼ French audiences are very verbal and appreciative if they like something—you clap for each number you like and make no noise at all for the ones you hate. If the outfit is a bomb, it's pretty easy to tell by this method. Stand when the collection is over and give the designer an ovation when he parades down the runway (which he will do only for the first two or three shows).

Naturally, the big trick is to get to an early show. To pull this off, you need to make the phone call yourself (the concierge can't do it for you) and be assertive and demanding without being too bossy or too *américaine*. You say something like, "I am in town from New York for just a few days and need to come in for the show tomorrow. I buy only Scherrer, you know." Or, "I AM coming tomorrow. What time is the opening? Please reserve me a seat." Make sure you mention that you plan to buy; no browsers at the big time. Some houses have just a few days of big shows and then show the line in private thereafter. This is no fun. Some houses have ten days of shows; after the first two or three days it is relatively easy to get in.

▼ Get there early for a good seat. Press shows have reserved seats (with celebs in the front rows and a distinct ranking by money and press power thereafter).

▼ Dress well.

▼ Don't forget to applaud.

If you have your eye on an outfit and happen to be the correct sample size (38), often you can buy the sample right after the show. You cannot take it home with you until the house is finished using it, but you can pay for it and consider it yours. When you come back for your private appointment after the show, ask your *vendeuse* to "put a hold" on the garment you fancy. When the garment is no longer needed for shows, it will be spruced up and altered for you—if need be. The house will ship and insure for you; you will get *détaxe*.

No one will ever know you have bought a sample. You can also order shoes and accessories this way, but you must be the size that the model wore. All items will be 50% less than the regular individual price. We still are talking about more than $100!

BALMAIN, 44 Rue François-1er, 8e. Tel.: 47-20-35-34.

PIERRE CARDIN, 27 Avenue de Marigny, 8e. Tel.: 42-66-92-25.

CARVEN, 6 Rond-Point des Champs-Élysées, 8e. Tel.: 43-59-17-52.

CHANEL, 41 Rue Cambon, 1er. Tel.: 42-61-54-55.

COURREGES, 40 Rue François-1er, 8e. Tel.: 47-20-70-44.

CHRISTIAN DIOR, 30 Avenue Montaigne, 8e. Tel.: 47-23-54-44.

LOUIS FERAUD, 88 Rue du faubourg-Saint-Honoré, 8e. Tel.: 42-66-44-60, 42-65-27-29.

GIVENCHY, 3-6-8 Avenue George V, 8e. Tel.: 47-23-81-36.

GRES, 1 Rue de la Paix, 2e. Tel.: 42-61-58-15.

HERMÈS, 24 Rue du faubourg-Saint-Honoré, 8e. Tel.: 42-65-21-68.

LACROIX, 73 Rue de faubourg-Saint-Honoré, 8e. Tel.: 42-65-79-08.

LANVIN, 15–22 Rue du faubourg-Saint-Honoré, 8e. Tel.: 42-65-14-40.

PER SPOOK, 18 Avenue George V, 8e. Tel.: 47-23-00-19.

REVILLON, 40 Rue La Boétie, 8e Tel.: 45-61-98-98.

NINA RICCI, 17 Avenue Montaigne, 8e. Tel.: 47-23-78-88.

BOUTIQUE YVES SAINT LAURENT RIVE GAUCHE, 12 Place Saint-Sulpice, 6e. Tel.: 43-26-84-40.

YVES SAINT LAURENT, 5 Avenue Marceau, 6e. Tel.: 47-23-72-71.

TED LAPIDUS, 35 Rue François-1er, 8e. Tel.: 47-20-66-40, 42-36-74-28.

SIDONIE LARIZZI, 8 Rue Marignan, 8ᵉ. Tel.: 43-59-38-87.

TORRENTE, 9 Rue du faubourg-Saint-Honoré, 8ᵉ. Tel.: 42-23-61-94.

EMMANUEL UNGARO, 2 Avenue Montaigne, 8ᵉ. Tel.: 47-23-61-94.

GUY LAROCHE, 29 Avenue Montaigne, 8ᵉ. Tel.: 47-23-78-72, 47-47-15-00.

HANAE MORI, 17–19 Avenue Montaigne, 8ᵉ. Tel.: 47-23-52-03.

PACO RABANNE, 7 Rue du Cherche-Midi, 6ᵉ. Tel.: 42-22-87-80.

JEAN-LOUIS SCHERRER, 5 Avenue Montaigne, 8ᵉ. Tel.: 43-59-55-39.

JEAN PATOU, 7 Rue Saint-Florentin, 8ᵉ. Tel.: 42-60-36-10.

Finds

ISABEL CANOVAS: Yes, she's the daughter of Manuel and Sophie, but she's also one of the major forces in the avant-garde. Isabel's specialty is accessories, as in gloves with gauntlet flares, seude insets, embroidery, and appliqué. She has a signature perfume that is a standout both for the fragrance itself and for the bottle it comes in. The shop is very tiny and dark, with display cases that make you appreciate the owner's talents as if she were an artist and this were her museum.

ISABEL CANOVAS, 16 Avenue Montaigne, 8ᵉ (Métro: Alma Marceau)

▼

LESAGE: Located in the Schiaparelli space on the Place Vendôme, so it doesn't have a sign you can watch for, Lesage simply says "Lesage" on the windows, with a pink "Schiaparelli" over it. But designer mavens have known for years that Lesage was the house that did all the beading for the couture. This new shop, with its "shocking" interior, where you sit at a little table and trays are brought to you, offers at retail a host of accessories at the highest prices in Paris. We're not sure what the real thing costs next door at Alexander Reza, but you might want to price it before you go in for some of these masterpieces. The work is sublime, but the price tags are not.

LESAGE, 21 Place Vendôme, 1ᵉʳ (Métro: Tuileries)

▼

SONGUER DAIYA: A high-tech space with tiny Christmas lights blinking out of the floors and everywhere. The clothes are expensive, hip, and made by a team of up-and-coming designers—like Nikita Godart and Laura Caponi. This is where you come to get the wardrobe you'll need when you become an Italian film star. Sunglasses start at $100, by the way.

SONGUER DAIYA, 245 Rue Saint-Honoré, 1ᵉʳ (Métro: Concorde)

▼

AU BAIN MARIE: Now in a new shop (they used to be right off Étienne-Marcel), this "kitchen" shop attract foodies, good cooks, and stylists who love to set a pretty table. You'll find antique linens, faience, and colored mother of pearl table settings that they sell in Barneys in New York for a lot more money.

AU BAIN MARIE, 10–12 Rue Boissy-d'Anglas, 8ᵉ (Métro: Concorde)

DAUM: Say "dome" to get it right—which is the way they've approached this new store. They certainly did everything right. While you may think of Daum and their large-size lead crystal cars, think twice now that they have this spiffy two-level shop and can display a lot of inventive glass art and colored glass pieces that will become collector's items.

DAUM, 4 Rue de la Paix, 1er (Métro: Opéra)

▼

LES OLIVADES: We were told that Les Olivades was started in the mid-1970s when someone in the Souleiado hierarchy departed and started a new firm. Indeed, Les Olivades reminds us of the Pierre Deux/Souleiado look, although the colors are more muted and pastel. While the goods are not cheap, they are about 30% less expensive than Souleiado right there in France. The store is small and a little hard to find—it's on a small street directly behind the Rue de Passy.

LES OLIVADES, 25 Rue de l'Annonciation, 16e (Métro: Muette)

Children's Clothes

BONPOINT: For classical styles, Bonpoint offers a museum setting for its perfectly crafted outfits. You've never seen anything so superbly made in your life. A simple smocked dress starts at $100, but prices can go to $300 for the grander stuff. If your child is over five, go upstairs where the more normal fashions are displayed. Parisian women of money and style swear by this resource.

There are several Bonpoint shops all over

town, by the way. Barneys carries the line in New York.

BONPOINT, 15 Rue Royale, 8e (Métro: Madeleine)

▼

DRAGON BLEU: A trendy shop for the *nouveau* style of kids' things that also has gifts, dolls, and all sorts of nice goodies.

DRAGON BLEU, 140 Rue du faubourg-Saint-Honoré, 8e (Métro: Saint-Philippe du Roule)

▼

TARTINE ET CHOCOLAT: Maternity dresses and layettes, French style, both classical and *nouveau.* Our fave: the big pink hippo in pink and white stripes sitting in a playpen and begging to be taken home to someone's child. There are Tartine et Chocolat boutiques in the major department stores.

TARTINE ET CHOCOLAT, 89 Rue du faubourg-Saint-Honoré, 8e (Métro: Concorde)

▼

MARINA: If you need couture for the tyke and the shoes to go with it, then rush over to these two stores, next door to each other. Clothes for infants to age six—ranging from blue jeans to party dresses. Many unusual styles of shoes.

MARINA, 82–84 Rue du faubourg-Saint-Honoré, 8e (Métro: Concorde)

▼

TIT': Although it doesn't look very inviting from the street, this is one of our major resources for classical styles, ranging from everyday dresses to absolutely magnificent dresses. Would you believe this store even has Chanel look-alike suits for your little one? There's more upstairs. Sailor suits galore for him and her.

TIT', 418 Rue du faubourg-Saint-Honoré, 8ᵉ (Métro: Concorde)

▼

PETIT FAUNE: Very original baby clothes in the *nouveau* style—some have matching shoes and hats. Everything is very, very small—up to size 2. The clothes are very American, and even the fanciest isn't in the classical style.

PETIT FAUNE, 33 Rue Jacob, 6ᵉ (Métro: Saint-Germain-des-Prés)

▼

ARDOISE: More reasonable French sportswear, with a good selection in many sizes. Lacoste for kids and much more. Good-quality, bread-and-butter items. Not far from Bon Marché.

ARDOISE, 33 Rue de Sèvres, 6ᵉ (Métro: Sèvres-Babylone)

▼

Don't forget the department stores—Bon Marché and Galeries Lafayette are famous for their children's departments. If you like cheap, fun, throwaway things, try Prisunic or Inno—each has a toy department and a good selection of inexpensive basics (underwear) and some acceptable ready-to-wear. Not terribly classy, but if you need just a bathing suit or a sweatshirt, why pay more than you have to? If you must have an Yves Saint Laurent dress for your little princess, buy it at Galeries Lafayette, where you can save the receipt and qualify for *détaxe*. Sonia Rykiel sells her children's clothes in her boutique. We do not think that Ungaro makes children's clothes. Oh, well.

Fabrics and Notions

I f you sew and want a taste of the couture, or a silly adventure, you may want to spend a few hours in the Marché Saint-Pierre area (18th *arrondissement*). You can combine this with a little tourist activity by walking up the back side of Montmartre to Sacré-Coeur, visiting the famous church, and then taking the funicular down. When you get out of the tram you will be in a neighborhood that sells fabrics, notions, etc. We talked to several design students from Esmond (the Parsons School of Design of Paris) who confessed to not one favorite shop but a careful perusal of the neighborhood each time they cut. Couture ends are sold; shopkeepers are friendly. Some working knowledge of French will be helpful. Cash. If you are going straight there, ask the taxi driver to take you to Marché Saint-Pierre, 2 Rue Charles Nodier, 18e. This will be a pricey taxi, by the way—the 18e is pretty far out. You can go on the *métro*, of course.

For a few other couture fabric resources, we stick our heads in at:

ARTISANAT TEXTILE, 21 Rue des Jeûneurs, 2^e

PARIS COUPON SOLDES, 18 Rue de Steinkerque, 18ᵉ
LA SOIE DE PARIS, 14 Rue d'Uzès, 2ᵉ
MENDÈS TISSUS, 140 Rue Montmartre, 2ᵉ
SEVILLA, 38 Rue de l'Annonciation, 16ᵉ

All of these sources are famous for couture fabrics—Chanel, YSL, Dior, the whole shooting match. Artisanat is in the Sentier, and also sells wool and yarn goods. Sevilla is right off Passy and is fabulous, if you hit it. As in most bargain shopping, luck counts. We've been to Mendès Tissus several times and have no idea what people are raving about. In theory it should be great—this is where the Mendès people dump their unused YSL fabrics. Of the several times we've been there, it has been boring. You just never know. (It's near Mendès, so it's worth a try.) Please remember that couture fabrics are not inexpensive—often they are $50 a yard for a silk that may not even be very wide.

China and Crystal

LIMOGES-UNIC: Limoges-Unic is a warm, beautifully appointed store with handsome wood cabinetry, antique chairs and desk, and help that speaks English. We've never had any problem with browsing or asking a lot of questions, even if we weren't buying anything. There are two stores: The first sells porcelain; the second is the gift part—with tiny china boxes, etc. Shipping is easily arranged; *détaxe*.

LIMOGES-UNIC, 12 and 58 Rue de Paradis, 10ᵉ (Métro: Château d'Eau)

▼

STE. LUMICRISTAL: This is one of our favorite shops because not only do they have great merchandise, but also we know they will negotiate on prices. We've been offered a 10% discount on our purchases (which totaled over $100); the store manager offered a gentleman who bought more than we did a 15% discount. The help is very friendly, there is a large selection of merchandise, and someone who speaks English will be glad to sit down with you and work out your order. They ship, accept U.S. checks, and will mail-order to you in the United States.

STE. LUMICRISTAL, 22 bis Rue de Paradis, 10ᵉ (Métro: Château d'Eau)

▼

BACCARAT: Entering the Baccarat offices in search of the shop is confusing the first time, since you must walk through the company's offices (in a magnificent, newly built glass building), go up some stairs and watch for signs that point out the museum (worth visiting) and the shop, which is to the left of the museum. The shop is a huge factory warehouse with red walls, set up with a bevy of computers that keep track of the quickly diminishing stock. Baccarat is six to seven months behind in its orders, so if they don't have what you want in the shop, they will send it to you . . . someday. Prices were similar to those at other outlets on the street, but there was an incredible amount of merchandise laid out on tables, reinforcing the almost overwhelming notion that all of it could be yours for bargain prices. They ship anywhere in the world and will mail-order. If there is breakage in your package, Baccarat will replace the item. *Détaxe*— but of course.

BACCARAT, 30 bis Rue de Paradis, 10ᵉ (Métro: Château d'Eau)

Makeup and Perfume Tips

You can go to any department store for discount perfume. You pay regular price at the store counter; you get a *détaxe* form from the store; you have it processed at the booth in the airport as usual; *then* you go to a cashier in the airport with your stamped *détaxe* form and get a cash refund right there in your hands. The good news is that you have it in your hands; the bad news is that it's in francs, you're rushing for an airplane, and you don't know what to do with it so you spend it on magazines. It's not a *bad* system, we just find it unnecessary. And you have to spend $180 or more.

▼ Makeup (even French brands) sold in the United States is made in the United States per FDA specifications—therefore contents and colors will vary between home and France. Names of products may be the same or different. Makeup with the same name will not be identical in shade.

▼ French perfume is made with potato alcohol (yes, you can drink it—just like Scarlett O'Hara) while Anglo-Saxon countries use cereal alcohol. This increases the staying power of the fragrance, as well as the actual fragrance—to some small degree.

▼ Many American brands you see in France are made in France (or Europe) for the European market—such as Estée Lauder and Elizabeth Arden. You may save on these items when *détaxe* is credited to your purchase. Revlon is always expensive, even in a duty-free, because it is not made in France.

▼ Pricewise, the best buy on beauty treatment programs is Clarins.

▼ If you ship your beauty buys, you automatically get a 40% discount; you need not buy 1,200 francs worth of merchandise.

▼ French perfumes are always introduced in France before they come out internationally. This lead time may be as much as a year ahead. If you want to keep up with the newest fragrances (about six come out each year, including men's) do what we do—get Catherine to ship you the newest items. Call the toll-free number (800-345-3964) and ask what's new, or ask to subscribe to the Born to Shop New Fragrance Club—for $100 you get two new fragrances a year; specify if you want ¼-oz. perfume size or large eau de toilette size. Shipping is included.

Other tips and makeup thoughts:

SEPHORA: This is a chain of cosmetics shops that now are all over France. We use the one on Passy, but you may bump into one elsewhere (such as the next time you are in Biarritz). Sephora is not a discounter like Bernard Marionnaud, and gives only the *détaxe*, not the duty-free price. But it is a huge shop, with counter after counter of makeup and a small department of underwear and panty hose in the far back. All brands are carried here, including our find of the decade, Bourjois (see page 149), as well as dime-store brands you have never heard of and big-name, hotsy-totsy lines. There's also a bath section where you can get some very nice bath gels for $10 a jar (the jar is heavy but makes a splendid gift) and bath crystals. It doesn't make sense for a tourist to shop here, because of the 20% duty-free discount you will forfeit, but many, many lines here are not sold in the duty-free stores—so you have to be the judge of whether you want to go to one of the best makeup stores you'll ever see.

SEPHORA

50 Rue de Passy, 16ᵉ (Métro: Muette)
66 Rue Chaussée d'Antin, 9ᵉ (Métro: Trinité)
38 Avenue du Général Leclerc (Métro: Alésia)

▼

BOURJOIS: Now then, about Bourjois. Many years ago, when we were snobs, we would not admit to anyone that we bought this cheapie makeup at Dames de France in Le Mans. When we found the line in Hong Kong, we mentioned it in our book, but in an offhand way. We were gaining in confidence. Then we heard from a friend at the television show *Dallas* that sometimes the head makeup man uses this brand, and we thought we were ever so clever to have discovered it. Then—get this—we heard from a big-name designer that Bourjois is made by the same company that makes the Chanel makeup, and is virtually the same thing. Now we're quite proud of having been the first on our block to try it. Bourjois is hard to find. Forget the duty-frees, forget the big stores. Buy Bourjois at any Prisunic; at Sephora or at Galeries Lafayette in Nice. Prices are the same in all retail outlets—about $5 for a blusher.

BOURJOIS MAKEUP, in department stores

▼

SHU UEMURA: He's one of the most famous makeup artists in the world. We don't care abut fame (anymore), but we do care about color. The hues are spectacular. If you consider yourself an aficionado of cosmetics, to be in Paris and not go to Shu Uemura is a sin.

SHU UEMURA, 176 Boulevard Saint-Germain, 6ᵉ (Métro: Saint-Germain-des-Prés)

GUERLAIN: Two insiders' bits of information: Guerlain perfumes are sold only through Guerlain stores, and are not discounted, but Guerlain makeup is sold through department stores and at Bernard Marionnaud. Note that only some of the fragrances are sold in the U.S.

GUERLAIN

68 Avenue Champs-Élyseés, 8ᵉ (Métro: F. D. Roosevelt)

2 Place Vendôme, 1ᵉʳ (Métro: Opéra)

93 Rue de Passy, 16ᵉ (Métro: Muette)

▼

ANNICK GOUTAL: Not far from Guerlain on Place Vendôme is Annick Goutal. This is a very Parisian, turn-of-the-century kind of place that creates its own scents. The packaging is elegant and refined; this just may be the perfect gift item to take home. Look for the inlaid mosaic tile on the sidewalk and march right in. We're talking about bottles with gold butterfly tops, fluted, curvy glass, and filled with perfume that smells like rainwater and rainbows. You can make a purchase in the $12 to $25 range that may be one of the hits of your trip.

ANNICK GOUTAL, 14 Rue Castiglione, 1ᵉʳ (Métro: Concorde)

Makeup Duty Frees

CATHERINE: We have spent many years and many trips working on the perfume and makeup connection, and have settled on Catherine as the best in Paris. This is a tiny shop that sells all fragrances and some cosmetics. They also sell big-name gifts like scarves, jewelry, etc., and a few designer-inspired items. We also think that Catherine (actually her son Jean-Pierre) offers the best deal in Paris. You get the maximum discount, and the *détaxe* is taken off your purchase price at the time of purchase, which is virtually unheard of anywhere else.

We rely on Catherine for several reasons.

▼ We know they're honest, which in a business like this is asking a lot.
▼ They do a huge mail-order business with the United States, and will provide you with easy-to-use forms and a toll-free phone number (800-345-3964).
▼ This is the best *détaxe* system in the business.
▼ Their flat discount of 40% is the highest you can find anywhere.

If you get there at 9:30 A.M., the store will be empty.

CATHERINE, 6 Rue de Castiglione, 1er (Métro: Concorde)

▼

RAOUL & CURLY: One of the most famous of the big-name duty-free shops, Raoul & Curly always is jammed and always gives us a headache. No discount in the world is worth fighting this mob. But they have everything, and a gigantic selection of cosmetics. We're talking floor-to-ceiling stock. Downstairs there're some gift items, such as men's shirts and ties and some women's handbags.

RAOUL & CURLY, 47 Avenue de l'Opéra, 2e (Métro: Opéra)

▼

MICHEL SWISS: Another of the fabulously famous duty-frees, this one is upstairs in a building whose elevator can take only three adults. In the high season, tourists stand in line in the courtyard just waiting to get into the elevator! The selection is immense; so are the crowds. This is a great resource for the person who may not spend much and wants to get *détaxe* without going to a department store.

MICHEL SWISS, 16 Rue de la Paix, 2ᵉ (Métro: Opéra)

Fun Jewelry

BURMA: If the real thing is beyond you, try Burma! There are a few Burma shops; we have been to them all and really insist that if you want to have fun while doing this, you stick to the Faubourg-Saint-Honoré shop. Burma knows how to make copies of important jewels. We're still sorry we missed out on the sapphire and diamond earclips that would have made us look exceptionally like Princess Di. We got a "Bulgari" ring with "diamonds" and a big cabochon "ruby" for about $125 with strict instructions not to wash our hands while wearing it. It's an excellent copy, however, and a classic.

BURMA, 72 Rue du faubourg-Saint-Honoré, 8ᵉ (Métro: Miromesnil)

▼

KEN LANE: Ken Lane has shops in Paris and London and continues to do well in the *faux* glitz business. His designs are almost obviously imitation and while very much the rage right now are not the kinds of things you buy if you want to fool your friends into thinking you've got the real thing.

KEN LANE, 14 Rue de Castiglione, 1ᵉʳ (Métro: Concorde)

▼

PEARL HOUSE: Is tucked in the back corner of a *passage* (French for arcade) and is worth finding if you are into do-it-yourself *bijoux* and the Ylang-Ylang glitzy look. They have jars and jars of unstrung pearls, beads, glitter, doodads, diamonds, and the like. Everything costs pennies; fixings also are available. No English, but you can do well with pointing here. It's open from 10:30 A.M. to 7:30 P.M. seven days a week, and is virtually next door to the Pompidou Center.

PEARL HOUSE is at Quartier de l'Horloge, 1 Rue Bernard de Clairvaux, 3ᵉ (Métro: Rambuteau)

Shoes and Leathergoods

ARCO: If you've had it with little LV's or even little MCM's on your tote bags and luggage, make your way around the corner from the Rue Saint-Honoré and onto the top part of Rue Cambon, near the Rue de Rivoli, not near Chanel. Step into Arco for sporty yet chic luggage that goes with the Ralph Lauren look. Prices are high but not exorbitant. You can buy a tote bag for a little more than $100 and have something handsome to show for it.

ARCO, 5 Rue Cambon, 1ᵉʳ (Métro: Concorde)

▼

STEPHANE KELIAN: This is one of our faves; check out the tiny shop at the Place des Victoires. Prices sometimes are half—we saw a pair of shoes in the United States for $225 that Kelian sold for $125. Kelian does young, slightly weird but chic shoes and is sold mostly through other shoe stores.

STEPHANE KELIAN, 6 Place des Victoires, 2ᵉ (Métro: Bourse)

MAUD FRIZON: Maud Frizon is made in Italy but designed in France and sold in a handbags-only shop on the Rue de Grenelle on the Left Bank and at a shoe store on the Rue des Saints-Pères, around the corner. Expect to pay $300 for a pair of shoes.

If you crave "Maudies" but find them out of your budget, try Miss Maud, or go discount (see Mi-Prix, page 129).

MAUD FRIZON
7 Rue de Grenelle, 7ᵉ (Métro: Sèvres-Babylone)
81–83 Rue des Saints-Pères, 7ᵉ (Métro: Sèvres-Babylone)
MISS MAUD, 21 Rue de Grenelle, 7ᵉ (Métro: Sèvres-Babylone)

▼

TOKYO KUMA GAI: If you are a true shoe aficionado, you've heard of this late, great man, Designs are less expensive in Paris, where they compete with Miss Maud in price ($150ish) —but are even a little wilder. Stop by to see genius in action.

TOKYO KUMA GAI, 52 Rue Croix des Petits Champs, 1ᵉʳ (Métro: Palais-Royal)

▼

CHARLES JOURDAN: Charles Jourdan has several large shops all around Paris; they also produce the Xavier Danaud line and the Christian Dior line, which are sold in their own shops. Danaud is the cheapest of the lines. Jourdan will cost less in France, but make sure you buy enough to qualify for *détaxe* to maximize your savings. One pair of shoes probably won't do it for you. Sales are excellent. Quite luxurious and expensive ready-to-wear as well as accessories and a fragrance are sold in most of the shops.

CHARLES JOURDAN, 8 Boulevard de la Madeleine (Métro: Madeleine)

TOP GRIFFES: Check out Top Griffes, where we've seen a lot of Jourdan sold for half the French retail price at this teeny shop that is open only from noon to 7 P.M.

TOP GRIFFES, 1 Rue de Marivaux, 2ᵉ (Métro: 4 Septembre)

▼

GIGI'S SOLDES: We also like this Italian shoe bargain basement on the Place du Marché Saint-Honoré, which (as you can tell from the street name) is an off-street of the Rue Saint-Honoré (although it's not really in the main-stream of everything) and has Italian-made French designer brands. We found Ungaro there; also Valentino, Yves Saint Laurent, RM (which is Givenchy), and some Maud Frizon look-alikes. We also saw an American department store (Nordstrom's) label in some shoes.

GIGI'S SOLDES, 30 Place du Marché Saint-Honoré, 1ᵉʳ (Métro: Pyramides)

▼

CHAUSSURES DE LUXE: Just like the name says, they sell deluxe shoes here. But discounted! They are last year's shoes, *mais oui*, but most of them are from Charles Jourdan. The store is tiny, the curved staircase down is even tinier, but there you can find Charles Jourdan silk scarves (the huge shawl size) for about $100 and even deluxe designer underwear.

CHAUSSURES DE LUXE, 2 Rue de l'Arc de Triomphe, 7ᵉ (Métro: Étoile)

Foodstuffs

I f you are looking for an inexpensive gift to bring home, consider putting together your own food basket. Foodstuffs are not necessarily easy to pack or lightweight, but they can be rather cheap and look like a lot once you get home and put them in your own basket or wrap in a clever fashion. We've done a selection of four mustards (total cost in France, $4.00) and given it as a gift to someone we would have given a $10.00 present to. Gourmet French mustards usually cost $1.50 to $2.50 each in the United States. The easiest place to do foodstuff shopping, and probably the cheapest, is at Prisunic or Monoprix. There's a Prisunic on the Champs-Élysées, and a Monoprix next door to Galeries Lafayette, so both are convenient to tourists. Check out mustards (we like the Maille brand in its many varieties), jams (Lenzbourg), or spices. You cannot bring back any fresh foods. Prices are slightly higher at Felix Potin, a chain of grocery stores much like Gristede's of New York, but you may want to dash in and out of any of the millions you will pass as you shop the streets of Paris. Our favorite Felix Potin is on Avenue Victor Hugo, across the street from Bottega Veneta. If you're more interested in the private brands, Fauchon and Hediard are both fun.

If you are a serious food freak, our section will just get you started. We cannot eat our way across Paris because then all our new clothes wouldn't fit.

If you plan on buying foodstuffs, save your plastic bags from shopping adventures or bring a boxful of Baggies with you. Wrap each jar or bottle in plastic and tie the top of the bag with a twist tie (they come in the box) before you pack the item. If the cushion provided by your clothes doesn't protect the jar, at least you won't get mustard all over your new suede shoes. Many of the big food stores will ship for you, but beware: Foodstuffs usually are very heavy. We have hand-carried olive oil, schlepped a bottle of cider through seven European cities, and held the *nouveau beaujolais* on our laps from Paris to L.A., so we know what dedication is—but we also know what heavy is.

These are some of our favorite, regular haunts; undoubtedly you will find your own, depending on what hotel you stay in. Needless to say, much food shopping for *le pique-nique* is done close to the hotel.

If you're bringing food back, remember that if it's alive—fruit, vegetables, meat products— it's *verboten.* Pickled or prepared foods are OK, as is anything in a sealed can. Chocolates filled with liquor are not.

FLO PRESTIGE: This is actually a small chain and also a catering service. They can cater for us any day. We buy prepared foods, cakes, and even ice cream here. They have their own line of soups and canned goods; we'd just as soon buy lunch or dinner. Their prepared meals will make you wish your hotel supplied your room with a microwave. We have used only the Opéra location, which is near the Meurice, but we trust the others.

FLO PRESTIGE

42 Place du Marché Saint-Honoré, 1er (Métro: Tuileries)

61 Avenue de la Grande Armée, 16e (Métro: Argentine)

102 Avenue du President Kennedy, 16e (Métro: Passy)

▼

G-20 COMESTIBLES: More like a fancy supermarket, G-20 is right smack in the middle of the Rue de Buci and the stalls and flowers and fresh produce and French charm you dreamed of. On a Left Bank visit, you can stock up from the vendors and the market and have a marvelous picnic at the church. If you don't want to shop at this type of grocery store, or from the vendors of fresh goods, you still are almost next door to La Boutique Layrac Traiteur for prepared foods.

G-20 COMESTIBLES, Rue de Buci, 6ᵉ (Métro: Mabillon)

▼

LA BOUTIQUE LAYRAC TRAITEUR: Anything from *boeuf bourguignon* to *pommes de terre au gratin* dished out in a container for your picnic or party. A fancy pigeon dish may be $10 for a serving, but the potatoes are only $4. Little is over $15, and we think the prices are quite fair. Who needs Tour d'Argent?

LA BOUTIQUE LAYRAC TRAITEUR, 29 Rue de Buci, 6ᵉ (Métro: Mabillon)

▼

GARGANTUA: Another of our regulars near the Meurice, Gargantua has cooked foods, wines, jars, and cans of fine eats. Only a block from the Tuileries; you can picnic in the garden if you like. This is a full-line shop, so you can get everything at one stop. They'll happily throw in free plastic knives and forks.

GARGANTUA, 284 Rue Saint-Honoré, 1ᵉʳ (Métro: Tuileries)

▼

FAUCHON: We often bring back tins of tea as inexpensive gift items. Prices are high here, and many of these items are available elsewhere (have you been to a Prisunic or Inno lately?), but it's a privilege just to stare in the windows. The salespeople also are extraordinarily nice. There are three parts to the store: Fruits and dry goods are in a mini–department store of many floors, prepared foods are next door, and the cafeteria is across the street. You buy a ticket, then get the food.

FAUCHON, 26 Place de la Madeleine, 8e (Métro: Madeleine)

▼

LENOTRE: We're LeNotre dessert freaks, but the store is a full-fledged *charcuterie*. You can get your picnic here, or your wedding party. They're open on Sunday (unusual) and will gladly guide you through any pig-out. For a price, they will deliver to your hotel.

LENOTRE, 44 Rue d'Auteuil, 16e (Métro: Michel-Ange Auteuil)

▼

FOUQUET: If asked to pick the single best gift item in Paris, we just might say it's the box of ten jars of goodies from Fouquet. Fouquet gift boxes are as heavy as they are famous, but the store will ship for you. There's no problem finding lovely gifts in the $25 to $50 range, but the shipping may double the price. The boxes are so extravagant that they look like double the price, so you do get some value here.

FOUQUET, 22 Rue François-1er, 8e (Métro: F. D. Roosevelt)

▼

HEDIARD: Conveniently located around the bend from Fauchon and Marquise de Sévigné, Hediard competes with the world-class food stores on its own. Hediard has been in the food biz since the mid-1800s, and there is little you cannot buy in this shop. They will also deliver, but room service may not be amused.

HEDIARD, 21 Place de la Madeleine, 8ᵉ (Métro: Madeleine)

Gifts

I f you're looking for name-brand status and fancy wrapping, any couture house (except perhaps Ungaro) or big-name manufacturer has an item for you. Sometimes you can find an item for $25–$30. Christian Dior specializes in these gifts; Nina Ricci has a niche for them; Christofle has a good selection of under-$100 items. You can find a leather case of Post-It Notes at Hermès for about $50. The famous scarf costs $130 on your airplane. For antique *bibelots*, try the Left Bank or Flea Market (see page 44); you will have no trouble whatsoever in this price range.

▼ If you are looking for a gift for the man who has everything, we suggest the boxer shorts with the little Eiffel Towers on them in pink and green ... about $15. If you run out of ideas for him (why is it that inexpensive gifts for men can be so difficult?), a bottle of Chivas Regal or Napoleon Cognac will be $15 to $20 in the duty-free as you leave France.

▼ There are not a lot of wonderful gifts that will thrill your kids. We're suckers for the Snoopy collection, which has T-shirts and/or sweatshirts that feature Snoopy and a slogan in French. Prices range from $15 to $25. Our main source is La Boutique, 5 Rue de Castiglione, right across from the Meurice, but many shops sell these, including the various Hallmark shops.

▼ We still like foodstuffs for gifts, and we regularly shop in grocery stores (Prisunic, Inno, Felix Potin) for unusual jams, mustards, oils, vinegars, or sweets. Sometimes we put together a food basket, sometimes we just bring a jar of mustard as a dinner gift. We are not experts on wine, so we avoid the fancy shops but do trust the Nicholas chain to provide us with a good wine to hand-carry back to someone who cares. In the fall, the *nouveau beaujolais* is ripe for tourists.

▼ If you want to stock up on gifts appropriate for anyone—man or woman—and any occasion, buy Rigaud candles. They are half the U.S. price in Paris.

8 ▼ PARIS ON A SCHEDULE

Tour I: All-Day-Killer-See-It-All Tour

1. Begin the tour at Galeries Lafayette, main store, on Boulevard Haussmann. They open at 9:30 A.M. (they're closed Sunday). Remember to save your purchase receipts for *détaxe* at the end of the shopping tour. Allow one hour. Be sure to see: designer circle; children's department (if you've got children or are very, very tiny); toy department; sport section; and luggage—you will need an extra tote after today.

   Collect your receipts and take them to the *détaxe* desk on the first floor. Allow fifteen to twenty minutes for the paperwork.

2. Now for perfume: Head down the Rue Auber toward the Opéra and visit Freddy (No. 10), or take the Rue Scribe (just south of the Rue Auber) to Bingo (No. 3).

3. Now that you smell wonderful and have bought all your presents, turn right and follow Boulevard de la Madeleine toward Place de la Madeleine. On the street, don't miss Charles Jourdan (No. 5), Bally (No. 11), and Rodier (No. 11). (Rodier is closed Saturday.)

4. From the Madeleine, stroll down Rue Royale, where you won't want to miss anything, especially Lalique (No. 11). Give yourself a half hour if you are a fast shopper. Otherwise, enjoy yourself and allow an hour. When you have bought everything you ever imagined you couldn't afford at Lalique ...

5. Walk away from the Place de la Concorde and to the Rue du faubourg-Saint-Honoré, where you should turn left. Since the *faubourg* has so many designer boutiques, allow two hours to walk and shop this street. About two blocks past the Élysée Palace, turn left on Avenue Matignon and proceed to Anna Lowe (No. 55). Follow Avenue Matignon to the Champs-Élysées, strolling on this famous street (toward the Arc de Triomphe) and crossing the murderous traffic in time to grab a cup of coffee at Le Drugstore—or the sidewalk café of your choice. With your fix of high-powered European coffee, you'll be ready to conquer the rest of the Champs-Élysées. Aren't you glad you bought that extra tote at Galeries Lafayette?

Tour 2: All-Day-Bargain Tour

1. Begin your day with a *croissant* and strong *café au lait*. Wear your most comfortable shoes, and take the *métro* to Franklin D. Roosevelt. From there, walk the Champs-Élysées to Prisunic, which is at the corner of Rue de la Boétie. Spend a half hour.

2. Taxi next to Nina Ricci (or walk from the Champs-Élysées to Rue Marbeuf to Rue François-1er to Avenue Montaigne). Nina Ricci is at 39 Avenue Montaigne. Then there's Christian Dior (No. 26). Spend an hour. (If an hour is too long, push ahead or add Isabel Canovas and Porthault—up half a block from Christian Dior—to your dance card.) Taxi to the next stop, or walk along Avenue Montaigne to the Place de l'Alma, where you will turn right on Avenue Marceau and proceed two blocks to our favorite bargain boutique, Babs.

3. Babs (No. 29) on Avenue Marceau. Plan on spending a half hour, and don't miss

the jewelry counter! When you are completely redressed and bejeweled, proceed by taxi to Réciproque. (This *is* walkable—but you'll be too tired to shop after you walk it!) (Take the 63 bus.)

4. Réciproque, 95 Rue de la Pompe. Spend a half hour—more if you are lucky. Don't miss their other shops up the street!

5. Next, walk north toward Avenue Victor Hugo, and turn right onto Rue Gustave Courbet, where you will want to see Caméléon (No. 13) and Ellipse (No. 26). Carry a small street map with you in case you get stuck, or ask directions as you go. If you do not speak French, merely point to our listing and its address and ask for guidance.

   If you are hungry, this is a good area to find a quick bite. If you are having too much fun, flag down a taxi and cross the Seine to the 14ᵉ. (It's easy to get cabs at the many stands on the Champs-Élysées.)

6. Have your taxi drop you at Eglise d'Alesia-Saint Pierre de Mantrouge. Take to the Rue d'Alésia, where you will find Dorothée Bis Stock (No. 76), Cacharel Stock (No. 114), Daniel Hechter Stock (No. 118), and others.

7. Taxi across the Pont Sully or Austerlitz to cross back over the Seine, and make a quick stop at Jean-Louis Scherrer, 29 Avenue Ledru-Rollin. Don't miss the fabrics downstairs! (If Scherrer does not make your heart go pitty-pat, skip this stop.)

8. Get another taxi (think of all you're saving on clothes!) to Mendès, 65 Rue Montmartre. Plan on spending an hour (if you are lucky). If it's a bad day at Mendès (and they happen), you'll be out of there in five minutes. Feeling hungry? You are in a great location for *crêpes* or fast food, as Mendès is near

the Forum des Halles and the Georges Pompidou Museum.

9. If you can still carry your packages, or even fit inside a taxi, grab one in front of the Pompidou (where they congregate) and proceed to Rodier Stock, 11 Boulevard de la Madeleine. Plan to spend a half hour.

10. As you wind down your day, move on to Gigi, 30 Place du Marché Saint-Honoré, where you can replace those shoes that by now have worn thin! Finish up with discount fragrance shopping at Catherine, 6 Rue de Castiglione, which happens to be next to the Hôtel Meurice. Collapse at the Meurice for tea—or something stronger.

Tour 3: Left Bank Discovery Day

Begin at Saint-Germain-des-Prés (a church) on the Boulevard Saint-Germain. Behind the church you will find a charming area for browsing, including open-air food markets, clothing stalls, bookstores, and art galleries. Walk the Rue de Buci, Rue Jacob (a famous street for antiques shops), Rue Bonaparte, and Rue de l'Abbaye. If you do the tour in a circle, you can end up back at Saint-Germain.

Back at Saint-Germain, walk the Rue de Rennes and explore also:

▼ Rue de Grenelle (Don't miss all the designer boutiques as well as antique shops. This street is especially stocked with good finds!)
▼ Rue du Dragon (This is a wonderful shopping street filled with unusual boutiques.)
▼ Rue des Saints-Pères (Maud Frizon is here.)
▼ Rue de Bac
▼ Rue du Four
▼ Rue de Seine

▼ Rue Bernard Palissy
▼ Rue Saint-Sulpice

See page 187 for an antiques tour of the Left Bank.

9▾ HOME FURNISHINGS, ANTIQUES, AND COLLECTIBLES

French Style

Man cannot live by couture alone—that's why the Hall of Mirrors was invented. It's undeniable that French influence has touched all levels of home design, from the royalist to the pleasant peasant point of view. While "Country French" is still a hot look that is considered "new," there was a time in the not so distant past when no self-respecting grandmother would have anything except Louis XVI in her living room. Even if Louis was long dead and all Grandmother could afford was cheap repro, the "Louis" was *de rigueur* when no one knew what else to do.

Those days are past now, and French design has broken out into a third, brand-new category. Yes, one can go for the "Louis" and the high regency this and that, or one can safely choose the antithesis—the plank wooden table, the *provençal* prints, a little faience; but more important, one also can choose nouveau French—the newest design look since Memphis Milano ran its course. For the first time in perhaps a hundred years, new home furnishings and decorating ideas are coming out of Paris. There are hot "new" French designers (led by a hot, "new" woman—Andrée Putman—who's been hot and new for about fifty years), and international eyes are looking to Paris for the latest definition of French style.

French style can be considered in three very different forms: classical French design; Country French design; and modern French design.

Classical French Design

Daydreaming of living in a French ancestral home filled with silken tassels that float off the furniture and sweep the parquet floors? Thinking it wouldn't be at all bad to contemplate life from an overstuffed dusty down pillow all done up in silk brocade (burgundy, of course) while you peer out the windows through antique lace curtains that dance in the gray sunlight filtered over the rose garden? Do you smell the freshly cut roses in their cut crystal vases scattered around the room, among the silver picture frames and precious *bibelots* standing—dust-free—on Empire end tables? If this is your dream, then you dream of classical French design.

In classical French design, everything is old and comes with a story. This is because classical French design is simply history—of the country, the family, and the generation that has cared for it and rearranged it. Many Americans come to France wanting to re-create classical French design in their own homes. They buy furnishings without understanding that you cannot buy history or pride or lighting. The light in France is very different from the light in New York and in most of the United States. Remember that lighting will affect the way the furniture looks in your home; the glow of France becomes a glare in California. Look at a good French painting and notice the quality of light—always muted and soft. Much French furniture is big and dark and looks gloomy in the wrong light. French architecture that emphasizes windows and muted light enhances big, dark furniture; if your home doesn't have the right kind of light, you can forget about getting the furniture, the fabric, and the color to look just the way they did in France. You can re-create a look and modify it to fit your home environment, but you never can recapture what took France centuries to build.

A Short History of French Design

The French design you love so much started with the Renaissance, when Italian, Spanish, German, and English styles and techniques were introduced into France and assimilated into the craft force. Seventeenth-century French furniture still shows the roots of its foreign origins—elements of design that disappear in eighteenth-century styles. You can begin to date the furniture you seek, or the styles of reproductions, by knowing the history and movement of the design trades, and the royalty that permitted the arts to flourish.

1515–47: François I was king during the early Renaissance, when tables became decorative objects; chairs took on the function of providing comfort; and beds were modified into exaggerated and extravagant designs, with posts and canopies.

1547–1610: The François I style continued with the ruling class and was carried through the time of Henri II, Catherine de Medicis, François II, Charles IX, Henri III, and Henri IV. But during this same time, the middle class began to modify these designs to fit their own life-styles, and French provincial furniture—now called country French—was created.

1610–43: With the reign of Louis XIII, the Renaissance ended and a new era of heightened design interest began, which sometimes is lumped together by nonpurists and called merely "the Louis." As begun with Louis XIII, the new design reflected the power of a day when artists and intellectuals were brought to favor and power. Cabinetry was designed with fully expressive carvings, tables became expandable, and chairs were designed with fully upholstered seats and backs.

1643–1715: Louis XIV improved upon earlier styles, refined them, and made them reflect the power and glory of his reign and of France. Fine furniture-makers were given positions of honor; many great names in the history of furnishings were born. This is called the Baroque period—which refers to the large size and exaggerated style of the carvings on most of the pieces. Symmetry, straight lines, bold carvings, fine marquetry, bronze appliqués, gilding, and the use of varnish and paint are indicative styles of Baroque furniture. Also during this time the sofa became a popular style, starting with what would today be called a daybed.

1723–65: Louis XV modified styles of the earlier period, and the Regency-Rococo look was born. Furniture became more simplified, soft, and almost feminine during this period. Regency refers to the period 1715–23, when Philippe d'Orléans ruled for Louis XV. Regency is a transition style that leads into Rococo, which took off when furniture became more curved and when Chinese and Japanese influence infiltrated the French classical designs. Veneers became lighter and more polished; rosewood suddenly was popular because of its light, delicate color, and the straight lines of the Baroque period completely disappeared when curves, spirals, ornaments, Chinese themes, painted this and that, gilding, ormolu, and inset Chinese plate or mirror became the rage.

1765–93: A Classical Revival grew out of a reaction to Rococo, as design once again returned to the straight line found in Greek and Roman architectural forms. Furniture took on an air of classical construction; fluted legs offset with bases, and feet that were designed like columns or capitals became the keynote of the look, and Greco-Roman ornamentation ruled the day.

1795–1804: (Directoire; Consulate) During the revolutionary period, furniture, art, architecture, and design were not of utmost importance. Symbols of the revolutionary government became part of ornamentation; fruitwoods were used, because of the difficulty of obtaining more exotic woods. The two styles, much more of the people than ever before, that emerged were Directoire and Consulate, named for the government forms. By the turn of the 19th century and the early years of that century, life was just getting back to normal, and design once again flourished. By the time Napoleon took over, France again was ready for pomp, circumstance, and high waistlines.

1804–15: Napoleon adopted the Classical Revival as his own style, and once again fine furniture was in style. Classical became the style of not just the ornamentation (lots of leaf clusters and acorns) but also the entire body form. Military symbols, including Napoleon's own (the bee and the letter "N") were gilded or appliquéd onto most pieces. Furniture became stiff, with the precision of a military drill. Comfort never was considered an issue.

Country French Design

Country French design was a spin-off of formal court furniture, made a little more accessible and even useful by the upper middle class. At the time of the multiple monarchies, France wasn't big in middle class— there were, almost exclusively, only rich people or poor people. But there were a few in-between tradesmen, craftsmen, and rather well-off country locals who were able to modify the styles of the royalty and use homespun fabrics to create a style of their own. While Louis XIII and Louis XV had a marked effect on country design, the French Revolution created such an antimonarchist feeling that more simple styles—of the people—suddenly were in vogue. Although Empire as a style, and Napoleon as an emperor, had more flash, the warmth of country style endured and did not take as much direction from Paris as before.

To some degree, Country French also reflects regional design. The people of the South of France are different in background (they are Mediterranean) from the people of Normandy and Brittany, whose ancestors remembered when Calais was part of Great Britain. While the current rage in Country French styles in the United States is based most on the southern and *provençal* imports, nuggets of pottery, faience, furniture, lace, and fabric from all over France complement the look. Paris offers a large collection from every region, but it doesn't hurt to get out and pursue your own path to the less-known countryside, where old pieces still can be found. They're in good condition, and they're an awful lot cheaper than they are in Paris—even if you shop at the Paris flea markets.

What we've come to love as Country French is a blend of the Italian influence created by craftsmen centuries ago, and the weather, and the local produce and products—walnut armoires that were carved to last for centuries, stone mantels, colorful handblocked fabrics of Indian inspiration, and tiles and pottery of a certain kind of clay. Country French has an exuberance to it that classical French style does not have, and this good nature has endeared it to Americans, who often combine French, American, and Scandinavian country looks in one happy mélange.

Modern French Design

S tudents of this sort of thing might classify
the beginnings of modern French design
as the Art Nouveau movement, which
gained popularity in about 1875 and was
in full bloom by the turn of the century. Art
Deco grew from Art Nouveau as the modern
look of the 1920s, but the future of design
seemed to go to the Viennese and the Bauhaus
School. After the Second World War, lean,
architectural furniture took the edge, and works
by Charles Eames, Harry Bertoia, and Eero
Saarinen were the frontrunners of the modern
design look. Italian design then took over and
was considered the enduring contemporary look
until just a few years ago—when suddenly,
quite unexpectedly, French designers grabbed
hold of the world's imagination and pocketbook. For the first time in over a century, the
world is looking to France for new ideas in
decor and home design. Even Harrods did a
series of room sets as a tribute to French home
decor and the new style last year.

The industry credits Andrée Putman with
the turnaround. Although Ms. Putman always
has been a well-thought-of and constantly
sought-after designer, she burst onto the international scene within the past ten years and
now is known to Americans outside the design
community. She has her own American licen-
sees, does some designs for Barneys in New
York, and proudly leads the Young Turks as the
arbiter of French taste and style.

In 1978 Ms. Putman opened Écart International, a furniture and design company that
brought back and produced classic modern
designs from the 1920s as well as new, classical
designs. She is largely responsible for the Retro
Deco look that is an insidious part of the
1980s look.

Meanwhile, French Minister of Culture Jack Lang made his support for young French designers very clear and, to the horror of many, modernized many French government interiors—starting with his own. He held a contest for new furniture design, chose four winners (Andrée Putman, Ronald Cecil Sportes, Philippe Starck, and Jean-Michel Wilmotte), and let them loose on offices that had not seen new design talent for over a hundred years. Today these four names lead the French design hit parade. Others to watch for are:

Christian Duc
Sylvain Dubuisson
Sacha Ketoff
Pascal Mourgue
Patrick Naggar
Daniel Pigeon
Janine Rocne
Pierre Sala

Hot Shops

If you want to look at some of this hot design work or see some of the individual items of furniture and tableware, you've but to poke your head in at Écart, or catch any of the following specialty galleries.

GALERIE NEDTU: Famous for its location in the Beaubourg, not far from the Centre Pompidou, Galerie Nedtu is very much in tune with the neighborhood and the times. If the street fashion doesn't give you enough clue as to what will be happening in the coming years, check out the new art and furniture in this gallery, which actually is adjacent to the Pompidou.

GALERIE NEDTU, 25 Rue de Renard, 4e (Métro: Hôtel-de-Ville)

▼

PAPYRUS: Aligne is the name of the New York showroom, if you care to buy the look wholesale in New York, which undoubtedly will be easier for you. But for the browser, designer, or thrill-seeker who just wants to enjoy the look, Papyrus is where you see the very square but eclectic collection of Jean-Pierre Cailleres that would be perfect in any New York Soho loft.

PAPYRUS, 31 Boulevard Raspail, 7e (Métro: Rennes)

▼

ARREDAMENTO: Arredamento sounds Italian and the look is similar; this is very modern lighting and furniture in the Milano mode. The public may buy from this showroom; they will ship to the United States. While the lighting groups are indeed something to write home about, beware of sending them. Some designs are hard to ship; we got an estimate on shipping a floor lamp that sent us reeling—$2,000 to fly it from Paris to JFK. This is high, but this is a serious business. If you do it, make sure the electricity can easily be converted for U.S. plugs. There are two addresses because the furniture showroom is in the 4e.

ARREDAMENTO
   29 Boulevard Raspail, 7e (Métro: Rennes)
   18 Quai des Celestins, 4e (Métro: Sully-Morland)

▼

ÉCART: Walk through the courtyard at 111 Rue Saint Antoine to a small door with a gray sign and there you are. See, you're not lost after all! Écart International is a widely celebrated design firm these days and is the brainchild of Andrée Putman. Timeless good design fills the showroom, and you marvel at chairs first designed in 1927 that seem as if they were hot off the sketchpad now. Putman spends most of her time doing interiors for rich and famous clients, but some of her furniture designs are sold here. Also there is work by Philippe Starck, who has the name everyone in design wants to drop these days. Écart will give you a list of American distributors if you prefer to worry not over *le shipping*. Should you buy in France, you will pay in French francs—at Écart, anyway—and qualify for an 18.6% tax-back discount when you export. Many models are not available in North America; ask.

ÉCART, 111 Rue Saint Antoine, 4ᵉ (Métro: Ledru-Rollin)

▼

FORMES NOUVELLES: Three floors of contemporary furniture in a building that you will stand in front of and shake your head while saying under your breath, "Are they crazy?" We aren't; you are if you miss it.

FORMES NOUVELLES, 22 Boulevard Raspail, 7ᵉ (Métro: Rennes)

▼

ÉDIFICE: This is a major showroom for design from both France and Italy, so you can see it all and compare the differences. Philippe Starck also has designs sold here, as do many of the hot young things.

ÉDIFICE, 27 bis Boulevard Raspail, 7ᵉ (Métro: Rennes)

NESTOR PERKAL: This is snuggled into a residential area in the Marais but is walking distance from the Place des Vosges and is well worth it to those who would walk a mile to say they've seen it all. The design talents of Nestor Perkal and Irena Rosinski are featured. The furniture has received rave reviews from the international design community in Paris. We particularly like the small accessory pieces that will pack in a suitcase or can be carried on the plane. We're such practical women. We flipped for the bright yellow and green table clocks designed like doughnuts, but if you find this hard to swallow, remember that we are the ones who bought a dozen miniature plaster chairs in Milan one year. There are many affordable accessories in the $50 range—they require care in transporting home, but they certainly will tell the world that you have an eye for high French modern style.

NESTOR PERKAL, 8 Rue des Quatre Fils, 3ᵉ (Métro: Saint-Sébastien Froissart)

Designer Saturday

A merican designers and housewives of style are familiar with Designer Saturday, an event held in New York to open the showrooms to the public and make access to the trade a little freer. Well, guess what, ladies! Paris also has Designer Saturday. It's billed as an international review of architecture and design, is sponsored by the Association for the Development of Design (that's our translation, not theirs), and is held in April—ask your concierge for the date this year, since the date varies each year. The first one was held in 1986, and sixteen showrooms participated. Most of them were the

young hot names we've already mentioned;
some others we didn't get around to, but they
are precisely the people you want to see.
This is just a day of contemporary design and
features furnishings, fabrics, lighting, and
accessories.

Decorator Showrooms

You are welcome to browse in decorator
showrooms to get ideas and widen the
scope of your personal visions, but don't
be surprised if many of the home furnishings fabrics suppliers want nothing to do
with you. Most showrooms have U.S. repre-
sentatives or distributors, and they do not want
to undercut their own agents. Some people
will tell you nicely that they cannot sell to you;
others will tell you rudely the same thing. But
every now and then you'll find someone who
wants your business. We cannot tell you who
does and who doesn't; poke your head in and
ask.

You should be able to negotiate a 10%
discount in a retail outlet that also functions
as a showroom, and an additional 18% tax
credit for *détaxe* on furniture. If you are
already in a showroom that is for the trade,
you will get only the 18% credit for *détaxe*.

JAC DEY: You can count on Jac Dey for really
good fabrics for upholstery—choose traditional
light geometrics, jacquards, florals, and French
patterns. Although there is a Dey showroom at
979 Third Avenue in New York, the prices
here are better—a good 20% below what similar goods would be if bought in the United

States. But the cost of shipping probably would equal the *détaxe* discount.

JAC DEY
  1 Rue de Furstemberg, 6ᵉ (Métro: Saint-Germain-des-Prés)
  3 Rue Jacob, 6ᵉ (Métro: Saint-Germain-des Pres)

▼

MANUEL CANOVAS: Our living-room furniture is upholstered from Canovas, but we weren't smart enough to buy it in Paris. While this showroom will not ship to you, you can take delivery in Paris (come back for your yardage in six to eight weeks). You can arrange for a shipper to take delivery if you want to take advantage of a magnificent 30% saving over U.S. prices. While Canovas is known as a fabric house, there are gift items and ceramics and things in the showroom. Expect to pay dearly for such *bibelots.* You may be paying $100 a yard for Canovas fabric, but you'll probably find it's worthwhile.

MANUEL CANOVAS, 5–7 Place Furstemberg, 6ᵉ (Métro: Saint-Germain-des-Prés)

▼

ROBERT FOUR: If you're thinking of a huge carpet—whether with a traditional tapestry pattern or something more *moderne*—you can buy directly from Robert Four, one of France's largest manufacturers. You will pay about $600 per meter for tufted carpet and over $1,200 for the Savonerie weave, but that's life in the big world of Aubusson. And, yes, you can also have your own portrait done in very, very small knots in a carpet that will last two hundred years.

ROBERT FOUR WORKSHOP SHOWROOM, 28 Rue Bonaparte, 6ᵉ (Métro: Saint-Germain-des-Prés)

NOBILIS: A classic-looking traditional showroom, Nobilis is one of those airy, modern spaces that could be anywhere in the world selling what it sells best. There are pads of paper and pencils, boards of fabrics and wallpapers—it's all just as you know it—but it's open to the public and is in the best location in Paris, right behind the church of Saint-Germain-des-Prés. In short, you do not have to be a decorator to buy. And buy you must. The fabrics are gorgeous, running from the palest of pastel cottons to the most brilliant silk moires. There is furniture just down the street—another good source. Shipping is no problem. You will thank us for the rest of your life for sending you here.

NOBILIS
   29 and 38 Rue Bonaparte, 6ᵉ (Métro: Saint-Germain-des-Prés)

▼

ÉTAMINE: If all those French Laura Ashley shops didn't convince you that the French love the English country look, one minute inside Étamine will. This is a crowded, fabulous shop filled with papers and paints and stencil kits and veddy, veddy English everything. They are the extensive agents for Colefax & Fowler, Collier & Campbell, Designer's Guild, Osborne & Little, and Charles Hammond. Shipping is not possible, but you will be so taken with what you see here that you won't mind going out and buying a steamer trunk. You get the 18% *détaxe*, of course. There is a showroom; a store for paper and paint; and a third store, for fabrics.

ÉTAMINE, 3 Rue Jacob, 6ᵉ (Métro: Saint-Germain-des-Prés)

▼

PIERRE FREY PATIFET: This is a boutique of fabrics, wall hangings, towels, bed quilts, luggage, purses, boxes, and table linens in a parcel of paisleys that is part Indian, part Aztec, and very French all at the same time. The look goes well with your basic Clarence House and Brunswig et Fils. They will not ship to the United States, but cash and carry will do the trick. There are two showrooms in New York (979 Third Avenue, 40 East 57th Street), two showrooms in Paris, and several showrooms all over Europe. You may want to consider buying a franchise yourself.

PIERRE FREY PATIFET
2 Rue de Furstemberg, 6ᵉ (Métro: Saint-Germain-des-Prés)
47 Rue des Petits-Champs, 1ᵉʳ (Métro: Bourse)

▼

ZUMSTEG: Although there really is a Mr. Zumsteg, the name refers to the fabric house that became famous when Yves Saint Laurent revealed that he chose many of his fabrics here. There also is a Zumsteg interiors line, which comes from the main offices in Zurich but which can be bought in Paris for much less than in the United States. The Zumsteg showroom in New York is at 979 Third Avenue. Most of the fabrics are extremely expensive and sophisticated. Those in the know, know.

ZUMSTEG, 4 Rue de Furstemberg, 6ᵉ (Métro: Saint-Germain-des-Prés)

Antiques

F rance has two types of antiques:

▼ genuinely old pieces of furniture; and
▼ reproductions of antique pieces of furniture
that may themselves be old pieces of furniture.

Whichever type you buy, remember that the
U.S. Customs people define an antique as something that is at least one hundred years old. If
the piece does not come with paperwork, you
must have a receipt or bill of lading from the
dealer that says what the piece is and its origin
and age. We won't tell you the tacky story of a
woman we know who tried to run four $100
Art Deco picture frames through Customs by
swearing they were a hundred years old. Customs officers do know their stuff. Art Deco
won't cut it for about forty more years. Good
luck anyway.

Buying Antiques

Anyone can buy antiques. Anyone can even
become an antique. But that's another story.
Antiques dealers are quite used to giving discounts to dealers—just present your business
card, act businesslike, and expect to take 10%
off the price. Even hoity-toity dealers—the kind
who never (well, hardly ever) haggle—give
the 10% to bona fide designers and decorators.

You also may be offered a kickback. If, as a
dealer, you buy a rather expensive item for
your client, the dealer may fix the price with
you and then—after the check has cleared—

give you back in cash a discount of 10% to 20%, which is considered your commission. The buying price has not been padded; you are not cheating your client. The seller is merely paying you an agent's fee for having chosen him. Naturally, he hopes to develop a relationship with you (through money, if not friendship), so that you will come back and buy more.

Reproductions

When the Industrial Revolution hit France, furniture began to be mass-produced. Furniture factories did not invent new styles but began to copy the older, established styles. New pieces often were made "in the style of." Much of this work is now over a hundred years old (you can date the start of the Industrial Revolution at 1860, more or less) and a lot of it is valuable, even if it isn't two hundred years old.

Antiques in Paris

Paris has all kinds of antiques—old ones, new ones, real ones, fake ones. Museum quality isn't hard to find—neither is Salvation Army quality and everything that comes in between. Important pieces do need permission to leave France. If you are planning on buying a very serious piece of furniture, you may need to hire a consultant, or stick to one of the shops with the international reps (where you will pay top-of-the-line dollars—and big antique prices always are quoted in dollars, by the way). If you are planning on having fun, you have come to the right city.

The expensive, museum-quality antiques are pretty much gathered in the tony little shops along the Rue du faubourg-Saint-Honoré. Only

Didier Aaron, which has a major reputation, is in the 16ᵉ.

Midrange antiques are scattered about town in various pockets of pleasure: the Left Bank; the *villages;* and the markets of Saint-Ouen.

Naturally, there are shops scattered everywhere in the city—but these are the main areas. Unless you collect a certain something, you'll probably have more fun if you wander in these areas and see the range of many shops rather than seeking out one address. Disregard this statement if you are a big spender and want to go to Didier Aaron. This is worth the taxi fare. Besides, if you have this much money, you probably brought your car and driver with you anyway, so what's one more stop?

If you suspect that you will be doing some serious shopping, read the section on shipping and make arrangements before you leave home. Should you just happen to walk into a shop and buy an armoire the size of the Jolly Green Giant because it calls to you, the shop probably will be able to help you arrange shipping. Or see our section on shipping for more hints. See page 26.

Any price paid for an antique should be arranged through careful negotiating. Even at Didier Aaron, you can ask if the price can be lowered. While you may not get much of a discount at Didier Aaron, a good bargainer who has found something a dealer wants to dump should be able to get a 25% to 30% discount from the asking price before the deal is finalized.

Museum-Quality Antiques

YVES MIKAELOFF: For tapestries from around the world and for important carpets, you must make an appointment to see M. Mikaeloff. He has a tiny showroom that displays a few items, but people who are doing this right will make an appointment to see the private collection.

YVES MIKAELOFF
10 and 14 Rue Royale, 8ᵉ (Métro: Concorde)

▼

GISMONDI: This is a gallery setting for the perfect collection of statuary, porcelains, and architectural pieces of the 17th to 18th centuries. The main floor is but a tease for the two floors above. Each one is more elegant than the next. Upstairs feels like a private museum, and you will weep that you are not a Rockefeller.

GISMONDI, 20 Rue Royale, 8ᵉ (Métro: Concorde)

▼

ARMAND AND SERGE KHAITRINE: A small shop with a top-drawer collection of 17th-, 18th-, and 19th-century pieces.

ARMAND AND SERGE KHAITRINE, 69 Rue du faubourg-Saint-Honoré, 8ᵉ (Métro: Concorde)

▼

L'AIGLE IMPERIALE ET LE SPHINX: The name says it all: Napoleon probably is buried under the floorboards. Paintings, armor, toy soldiers, swords, furniture par excellence. They buy, they sell, they appraise, they make war toys worth taking off your list of no-nos.

L'AIGLE IMPERIALE ET LE SPHINX
104 Rue du faubourg-Saint-Honoré, 8ᵉ (Métro: Miromesnil)
3 Rue de Miromesnil, 8ᵉ (Métro: Miromesnil)

▼

WISEN: This is a small shop with unusually large pieces. We once happened upon a set of four columns taken from a theater and done in Art Nouveau with gold leaf and all sorts of incredible detailing.

WISEN, 102 Rue du faubourg-Saint-Honoré, 8ᵉ (Métro: Miromesnil)

▼

ALEXANDRE POPOFF ET CIE: An unusual collection that combines porcelain figurines, teacups, and vases with a large collection of Russian antiques. The shop was opened in 1920 and served as a main dealer for émigrés who raised cash by selling off the family antiques. M. Popoff deals with museums, dealers, and even movie companies. Great fun.

ALEXANDRE POPOFF ET CIE, 86 Rue du faubourg-Saint-Honoré, 8ᵉ (Métro: Miromesnil)

▼

JEAN LUPU: Very fine, very fancy, very authentic, very Parisian, very much out of our price range.

JEAN LUPU, 43 Rue du faubourg-Saint-Honoré, 8ᵉ (Métro: Concorde)

▼

PIERRE ANDRIEUX: Be prepared for twittering when you walk in. The shopkeepers are two wonderful, older French ladies who go with the antique silver they specialize in. Don't pass it by as too pricey; you can get small gift items for under $20.

PIERRE ANDRIEUX, 66 Rue du faubourg-Saint-Honoré, 8ᵉ (Métro: Miromesnil)

▼

LE FORTIER: The family château deserves a tapestry from Le Fortier. If you can't afford one today, perhaps you'd care for a pillow, for about $100—which happens to be an excellent buy.

LE FORTIER, 54 Rue du faubourg-Saint-Honoré, 8e (Métro: Concorde)

▼

MAURICE SEGOURA: Perhaps this shop should just be declared a museum and charge an admission fee. The pieces contained in the two floors of this shop are of top, top quality. The specialty is 17th to 18th centuries.

MAURICE SEGOURA, 20 Rue du faubourg-Saint-Honoré, 8e (Métro: Concorde)

The Left Bank

We divide the Left Bank into three areas for antiquing: Saint-Germain; behind the church; and the fashion areas.

The shops with addresses on Saint-Germain may be a tad more expensive than the others, because they are paying higher rent. It's not that big a deal; we just thought you'd want to know. Many neighborhood shops belong to an association called Association des Antiquaires at Galeries d'art du Carré Rive Gauche. You can call them and ask when their next block party is—usually they have one every spring. Their 120 different shops each contribute one gleaming item to make up a show. On opening night musicians in costume stroll the streets, and everyone has an exceptionally good time.

The stores in the association are all on:

Quai Voltaire
Rue de Saints-Pères
Rue du Bac
Rue de Lille

Rue de Verneuil
Rue de l'Université
Rue de Beaune

They print a brochure that lists everyone's name and address; simply phone and ask them to send you one. If you can't see them all, here's our ranking, in order of preference, made as serious shoppers. If you're just looking, any old place will offer you charm and selection.

If you plan to spend your inheritance, do so in this order:

1. *Quai Voltaire:* This is the main drag along the Seine with the bigger shops that sell the fancy and high-quality items, many of which could almost make it to the Faubourg Saint-Honoré.

2. *Rue des Saints-Pères* and *Rue de Beaune:* There're about sixty shops along these two streets, and we're talking just antiques now. We won't mention that this also is great ready-to-wear and shoe territory. Some of these stores offer high-quality antiques; others offer the medium. It takes all kinds.

3. Other Directions: All of the other streets have between ten and twenty shops on them, with mixed quality. We're wild for the Rue Jacob, but there's nothing wrong with any of the other streets, either. Just weave from one to the next. Don't miss the cute little Rue de Furstemberg, which is so tiny it isn't even part of the association.

The other shops you'll find in a catch-as-catch-can manner— you wander around and one day find someone who sells fabulous Japanese armor you didn't know was there. You'll never be able to shop them all, but you can try!

Behind the Church

We can't begin to tell you all the good places behind the church, but since these don't belong to any association, we'll just give you a gentle shove:

BROCANTE STORE: This is a nice store for gifts, with its woody, cluttered interior. Every inch of space is covered with something to buy—glass paperweights, ceramic dogs, old brass picture frames, flasks, inkwells, bottles, compasses, old telephones—everything.

BROCANTE STORE, 31 Rue Jacob, 6ᵉ (Métro: Saint-Germain-des-Prés)

▼

FRANÇOISE THIBAULT: Country French; Country French; Country French.

FRANÇOISE THIBAULT, 1 Rue Jacob, 6ᵉ (Métro: Saint-Germain-des-Prés)

▼

MAUD BLED: Art Deco heaven right here on the Rue Jacob. Marvelous small items that make easy-to-pack gifts. The furniture also is good, but this is the store for gift items. Prices are considerably higher than at Saint-Ouen, beginning at around $100, as should be expected.

MAUD BLED, 20 Rue Jacob, 6ᵉ (Métro: Saint-Germain-des-Prés)

▼

GALERIE 13 RUE JACOB: This dark and musty shop adds to the romance of the antique chess and backgammon pieces.

GALERIE 13 RUE JACOB, 13 Rue Jacob, 6ᵉ (Métro: Saint-Germain-des-Prés)

L'APARTMENT: If china, glass, crystal, and linens are your thing, you will go nuts here. They had to take us away in chains. Mostly Victorian period pieces—ivory-handled knives, antique lace—but some things from the 1930s and 1940s.

L'APARTMENT, 21 Rue Jacob, 6ᵉ (Métro: Saint-Germain-des-Prés)

▼

LAURE WELFING: A very *art décoratif modern* shop, with an unusual sense of humor exhibited in the choice of items for sale. It's just a fun shop.

LAURE WELFING, 30 Rue Jacob, 6ᵉ (Métro: Saint-Germain-des-Prés)

▼

GALERIE ARTEL: Impressive collection of icons and religious art. The walls are deep red, which sets off the gold in the icons.

GALERIE ARTEL, 25 Rue Bonaparte, 6ᵉ (Métro: Saint-Germain-des-Prés)

▼

DAVID: Silver boxes, animals, baby teething rings, and the most elegant pitchers, candlesticks, and picture frames. A wonderful shop for silver collectors or wedding gift seekers, but prices begin at $100.

DAVID, 27 Rue Bonaparte, 6ᵉ (Métro: Saint-Germain-des-Prés)

The *Villages*

No, not the quaint little villages all over France where you know you can get good antiques, but the *villages*, the buildings that house many antique dealers under one roof. If you need a rainy-day-in-Paris occupation, a trip to any *village* probably will do it. But we don't need excuses to be indoors all day, after all—it saves time if you don't have to run all over town tracing down different dealers. Some *villages* are better than others, so listen, my children, and you shall see.

VILLAGE ST. PAUL: This can be a little hard to find if you aren't patient, since there is no one building named Village St. Paul or anything like that. This is a block or so of antiques dealers crammed into a small space between the Seine and the church of St. Paul, very close to the Marais and to the Bastille. Get off the *métro* at St. Paul and walk toward the river. What you'll find is a virtual warren of medieval streets and buildings, each housing antiques dealers. Hours are generally Thursday–Monday, 11 A.M.–7 P.M. There are many shops to wander, but try such addresses as 25 Rue St. Paul (l'Espace Temps) and 23 Rue St. Paul (Revisited) to get you started. Prices can be steep, but the variety of the merchandise, combined with the charm of the neighborhood, make this a delightful way to get lost in time. A good stop to piggyback with your visit to the Marais.

VILLAGE ST. PAUL, Rue St. Paul, 4ᵉ (Métro: Saint Paul)

▼

LE LOUVRE DES ANTIQUAIRES: This "store" is a department store of some 250 dealers. If you ask us, you can find everything you need right here. Indoors is a restaurant and a shipping agent and everything you'll need to make your stay here complete except for a mattress. They have shows devoted to a subject if you want to take in a little culture while you ogle; there is a program with everyone's name, booth number, and private phone. There's nothing to do here except wander and differentiate between the specialty dealers (silver, silver, silver) and the eclectic dealers. Life is hard when you have this much choice and so little money—or space. Conveniently located right across the street from the Louvre, this is your kind of place.

LE LOUVRE DES ANTIQUAIRES, 2 Place du Palais Royal, 1er (Métro: Palais-Royal)

▼

LE VILLAGE SUISSE: No gnomes here hammering at little pieces of chocolate or making watches, just a lot of dealers in the midrange to high-priced area with some very respectable offerings. There are 150 shops in an area one block long and two blocks wide. The Swiss Village is near the Eiffel Tower and l'École Militaire, but don't be getting your hopes up for cute or quaint—it's just two sets of modernish buildings and one old one. Prices are not outrageous, and most stores offer shipping.

LE VILLAGE SUISSE, 54 Avenue de la Motte-Picquet, 15e (Métro: La Motte-Picquet)

▼

LE BON MARCHÉ: Le Bon Marché is indeed a department store, and there are antiques in both parts of the store. On the second floor of Magasin 1 is the plebeian section, used goodies that are quite affordable; it's poorly displayed in the middle of the furniture section, so you may have trouble locating the area. In Magasin 2, walk in toward the grocery store and take the escalator on the right to the first floor, which is a flea market of antiques dealers. Each boutique is separately owned. You can find many good buys for under $100 in the approximately thirty-five stalls here. There is no *détaxe* on antiques.

LE BON MARCHÉ, 38 Rue de Sèvres, 6ᵉ (Métro: Sèvres-Babylone)

▼

LA COUR AUX ANTIQUAIRES: Housed in a crumbling but quaint New Orleans–style building, the eighteen small shops in this village are on three levels. Many are closed on Monday in the summer.

LA COUR AUX ANTIQUAIRES, 54 Rue du faubourg-Saint-Honoré, 8ᵉ (Métro: Concorde)

The Markets of Saint-Ouen

Also known simply as the Marché aux Puces, or the famous Flea Market, Saint-Ouen is comprised of several different markets, each with its own kind of dealers and each with its own special feel. We like them all, and while we find that some markets change, the area is steadily reliable for the best selection and the best prices on antiques and used wonders of the world in Paris.

▼ Marché Biron and Marché Cambon are the best markets for very good antiques. You'll see furnishings in various states of refinish and find dealers in various states of mind—some know what they have and are very hard-nosed about it; others want to move out the merchandise and will deal with you. They are particularly responsive to genuine dealers who know their stuff and speak some French. But not to worry; this is big business. At Biron they even take plastic. If you like good goods, start with Biron, then work Cambon. You may want to pass up the rest of the market. Cambon has about forty shops with two floors of very,

very nice 17th- to 18th-century furnishings, including many big pieces. The dealers at Cambon are older, so the market has a staid, almost refined air to it. This is a place for serious collectors, not fun-seekers. The dealers all sit around chatting amongst themselves, drinking their coffee, and reading the paper, and they seem bothered if you so much as ask a price. Be brave. Ask anyway! Biron has more activity than Cambon and is the primary market for dealers. Our friends Mike and Elaine turned us on to a dealer they trust who also works with American dealers (dealers only, no tourists, sorry); you'll know him by his Amherst sticker on the stall—Jean-Yves l'Homod, Stand 66, Alley 4. Biron is an indoor-outdoor kind of market with open walkways but covered stalls. Our favorite shop here is Les Verres de Nos Grande Mères; Mike and Elaine have bought big pieces from l'Homod, who also sells Pierre Deux and other big-name American dealers.

▼ Marché Serpette is our personal favorite for "finds" at good prices. These dealers take plastic and are eager to make a sale. This market is in a real building, not a Quonset hut. There is carpet on the floor, and each vendor has a stall number and a closing metal door. There also are large, nice, clean bathrooms on the second floor. Our favorite shop here is Costey-Roggerone (Stand 2, Alley 3), which specializes in tableware from 1930–40. They sell to Barneys and Bergdorf Goodman.

▼ Marché Paul Bert surrounds the Marché Serpette in three alleys that form a U. This market is outside and inside with lower-end merchandise, including Art Deco, *moderne*, and country furniture. Most of the items here have not been repaired or refinished. There could be some great buys here, but you need to have a good eye and to know your stuff.

▼ Marché des Rosiers is a very small market specializing in the period between 1900 and

1930. There are about thirteen small stalls in an enclosed building in a U shape.

▼ Marché Malik is famous for its *fripes*—used clothes. We've seen better elsewhere, but the range is mostly 1940s–1950s things. In years gone by we have bought good whitework here—no more. We think the best stand in the market is Lili et Daniel, which sells buttons, buckles, feathers, cuff links, cigarette holders, earrings, old purses, etc. You can buy wholesale by saying the magic words *en gros*.

▼ Marché Jules Valles is right down from Malik and is in a Quonset hut. Honest. This is a market of small-collectibles dealers who sell things such as toy trains, bottles, prints, and silverware. Mostly low- to mid-quality, and it's not terribly appealing. We thought the old postcards were the best buys.

▼ Honoré Paris is a new market open every day except Tuesday and Wednesday. It's a redone warehouse, with forty-two boutiques—some wild and wacky designer furniture, and many Art Deco and 1950s items; outrageous and fun, and a nice reprieve from the serious antiques.

▼ Marché Antica also is new—it's just a little-bitty building refinished in the Memphis Milano teal-blue-and-crème look. This market is filled with cute shops selling small collectibles of good quality at pretty good prices.

▼ Marché Vernaison is out the side entrance of Antica, and is more a glorified alley than anything else. It specializes in baubles, bangles, and beads. The trimmings shops have some very good prices. Another shop specializes in door knockers. The alley winds around in a triangular shape and the place is plain old-fashioned fun.

Shipping from the marchés: On Saturday only, a shipping agent, Camard, is inside the Marché Paul Bert. This office will do everything for you. They have a reliable reputation. Otherwise, the more established shops will make shipping arrangements directly for you.

Expect to pay $10,000 to ship a container from the market to the United States; a container has thirty cubic meters of storage space or room for about a hundred pieces of furniture. This is not a special market price, by the way, but the going price on any shipping line. You can get lower prices on groupage rates if you don't have a hundred pieces to send or can splurge on air cargo—if you are a wild and crazy thing and can't wait a few months for delivery. (Métro: Porte de Clignancourt)

Auctions in Paris

HÔTEL DROUOT: If you prefer your used furniture to come by way of an auction house, have we got a place for you! In Paris the auction business is tightly controlled and one house—the Hôtel Drouot—has all the business. Some ninety auctioneers are here, and several auctions will go on simultaneously (we've actually seen shoppers run from one room to another). The ninety auctioneers are all shareholders—equal partners—in the business, and in that sense the place is run much like a law firm. Speaking of lawyers, there are lawyers in France who specialize in auctions, because this is a very, very different business from the one we know and love in the United States and the United Kingdom.

Auctions are held every day except in summer, when they are not held on weekends. The auctions always begin at 2 P.M. and go until concluded, usually about 6:30 P.M. Previews are on Wednesday until 11 A.M.

Drouot is a weird and fascinating place. At the entrance, an information counter had catalogues and notices of future sales. Three TV sets on the ground floor show different parts of the building, and there is an appraiser who—free of charge—will tell you if an item you walk in with is worthy of auction, and then will appraise it for you. The estimate is done in a small, private room. If you agree with the estimate, you can set a date for your auction. The seller pays an 8% to 10% commission to the house.

The auction rooms are of various sizes; some can be divided or opened according to need. All the rooms are carpeted; art and/or tapestries are on the walls. The clients sit on chairs to watch the bidding; paddles are not used. Most of the clients are dealers; we have never noticed a very jazzy crowd here, even when we went to a Goya auction. All business is in French; if you are not fluent, please bring your own translator or expert, or book a translator ahead of time. (Call 42-46-17-11 to arrange for a translator.)

You needn't register to bid; anyone can walk in, sit down, and bid. You can pay in cash up to 10,000 francs. French people may write local checks; Americans cannot write checks. If you have only American money with you, there is a change bureau in the house. If you pay in cash, you can walk out with your item. If you pay by check, you must wait for it to clear. Shills occasionally are used by some dealers to up the price. Auctioneers are familiar with all the dealers and could possibly choose to throw a piece their way; the dealers may pool on an item. It's a dirty little business out there in the big, bad world.

You are responsible for shipping; there is no shipping office in the auction house. You start paying storage charges after twenty-four hours.

All auctions have catalogues, and the lots are numbered and defined in the catalogue.

You do not need a catalogue to enter a preview or an auction, as you do in New York. The conditions of the sale are plainly printed inside the first page of the catalogue (however, they are in French only).

If the basic auctions at the Hôtel Drouot are too fancy for you (we doubt that they are!), you may want to try the house's cheapie branch—Drouot Nord. Here you can pick up used household items and the kind of things people let go when a loved one has died and they don't know what to do with the estate. You also might get office furniture, unclaimed items held by French Customs, bankruptcy sales, tax sales, etc. If you've just moved to Paris to live in a garret, be poor, and write your great American novel, at a resource like this you'll pick up everything you need to start life. Serious antiques hunters will not be impressed. In fact, they will be depressed. Auctions are held every day of the week (no weekends) at 9 A.M.; there is viewing only for fifteen minutes prior to the sale.

Not to be outdone by the washtubs, the house has yet another branch—Drouot Vehicules, which auctions off used cars. There are two different locations in Paris; there is a preview the morning of the sale, and you must arrange a bank credit to pay if you do not have a French checking account. As in other branches of the house, you may pay the first 10,000 francs in cash. The cars are used cars driven by French government executives or by people who did not pay their taxes or car payments. They are in pretty good condition—it's sort of like buying a used car from Avis or Hertz. The house specialty is big, expensive cars, since these are the ones that people default on most regularly. The cars will be driven in the preview, and you are invited to kick the tires, but you cannot drive the car yourself during the preview. If you are considering buying a car here, driving it all over Europe, and then bringing it home, find out what modifications must be made on the model to meet U.S. standards. The cars that most Americans pick up at factories all over Europe and bring home are made for the American market. The cars at Drouot are real-live French cars.

HÔTEL DROUOT, 9 Rue Drouot, 9ᵉ (Métro: Le Pelletier)

DROUOT NORD, 64 Rue Doudeauville, 18ᵉ (Métro: Château Rouge)

DROUOT VEHICULES

17 Rue de la Montjoie, 93210 La Plaine Saint-Denis (north of Paris)

30 Rue des Fillettes, 93399 Aubervilliers (a suburb of Paris)

10 ▼ SOUTH OF FRANCE

Welcome to the South of France

Never before has it been so easy to explore the rest of France; to get out of Paris and go for it, to see for yourself what everyone has been raving about—and, while you're at it, do a little shopping.

Prices on ready-to-wear—actually, on everything—are higher in the South. This is, after all, the country's resort capital. But never mind. You've already been to Paris and bought your makeup, you've been to the stock shops and the designer shops—now you're ready for the local stuff and a great big dose of cute shopping. Not only the Côte d'Azur awaits you, but our own interpretation of the South of France, a state of mind as much as a state of being. Our South of France stretches from Marseille to Menton and beyond—in either direction. Give us a map and we'll show you a store.

This is our version of a vacation. Some people like to plop down in one place and stay there. This book can be used by them as beach reading. Others like to go, get lost, and then get found. More power to them.

We're shoppers; we're adventure seekers. We want constant visual stimulation, and we like to keep on moving; we're going to give you a little bit of everything in just a few days. Obviously you don't have to go at our speed. Nor should you. This isn't a race. So pick and choose to your own amusement, drive very carefully, and make sure you buy an extra suitcase at the Auchan (local K Mart) outside of Nice. We're about to guide you through paradise, and that means shopping bargains galore.

Booking the South/1

There are many guidebooks on the South of France, as well as many nonfiction books on travels, choices, and memories. Our tour includes three different sections of the area: Provence, Esterel, and the Côte d'Azur. So make sure your guidebooks cover all these areas. *The American Express Guide to the South of France* is pocket-sized and gives you everything you need in tight, tiny type; it is the book of choice for us.

Gault Millau does publish a Côte d'Azur edition, but it is not translated into English. It is best on restaurants and hotels (from Marseille to San Remo), and not great on shopping, but may be worth a browse while you're in the bookstore in Cannes.

Manston's *Flea Markets of France* has a rather complete listing of local markets throughout the country, if you want to take in more cities than we have in our tours or to coordinate your trip to different market days. We're geared for market day in cities we visit, but if you want to take on more, Manston's is the guide to help you.

Booking the South/2

There are a few ways to tackle hotels in the area; they depend not only on budget but on personal style. When we think of the coast, we think of opulence and sunshine and turquoise carpets, so we always go with Loew's. (The Monte Carlo location even has a shopping mall complete with our favorite big names: Dior, Chinacraft, Fred, Pierre Cardin, and others.) If you are looking for something more discreet or charming, perhaps you should try the hotel broker we trust on these matters, Jacques de Larsay (800-223-1510), who can book you in any class or budget in style.

Getting There

There's no shortage of ways to get to the South, from nonstop flights from New York to Nice (in season only), to regular commuter flights from Paris to Nice with their own quick-change terminal. Buy an Air Inter pass for a fixed dollar rate (under $250) and get seven days' free travel anywhere within France during a thirty-day period—this pass must be bought in the United States, so plan ahead.

If you'd rather not fly, enjoy the deal of the century when you climb on board the new Avis/SNCF (French National Railway) promotion called Rail N Drive France. For a flat price that is so small you'll laugh (we paid $129 each) you get four days of unlimited train travel anywhere in France and three days of unlimited mileage in an Avis rental car—you have fifteen days to do the traveling, or you can buy a bigger package that gives you fifteen days to travel in a thirty-day period. You do pay extra for the couchette on your sleeper train, but you will save hundreds of dollars. (We saved approximately $500!) Avis has this very well organized, and there are rental agents and drop-off points in train stations all over, including Monaco. Please note the second greatest blessing of this service: Avis is inside the station, not across the street or around the corner. There isn't a better buy in France. Call

800-AF-PARIS for details. We bought our passes in New York and still can't get over our good luck. VAT is included in this package price!

Car rental prices without special packages are expensive, especially if you don't get an unlimited mileage package. You may have to pay $100–$150 a day for a car if you drive as much as we do. VAT taxes on rental cars in France—28%—are additional, unless you have a package, so watch out.

Getting Around

I f you use the Rail N Drive package, you'll be able to conquer all the hill and coastal towns of the South with your little rental car and enjoy the benefits of unlimited mileage. We do warn you that some of these hill towns are very hilly, and if you are a nervous driver, you might want to consider coastal routes.

You can do a modified version of our tours by using only the train. You'll have to pick and choose carefully, and you won't get in as much, but you won't be stuck in traffic either. In-season (summer) traffic is frustrating and infuriating; consider sticking to the beach or day-tripping via the rails. There are also motor-coach trips for tourists, which offer you air-conditioning and tour guides, although these tend to be expensive and very touristy. One such trip may just make your summer ... and it does let someone else worry about the traffic.

Don't forget getting around on foot. While you really aren't going to walk from Cannes to Antibes, make sure you have on your sensible shoes. We can, and do, walk from Loew's La Napoule into Cannes (it justifies a big dinner); old cities are often paved with cobblestones, and parking places are hard won.

If you are driving, don't forget to check on local parking regulations. Most of the cities in the South have a system whereby you buy a ticket from a meter and then place the ticket in your windshield (inside, not out) to indicate how long you have paid for the spot. Just because you don't see a conventional parking meter, don't assume that the space is gratis.

While most roads and cities are well marked, as you approach a town, always take the directions for *Centre Ville*. As we prowl the South, we are looking for the old towns; we don't care about shopping in the burbs or the upper city of Cannes, etc. You probably don't either.

"Casino" Shopping

The roads of France are dotted with what are called Commercial Centers. Such delights are usually found outside a big city, but can be anywhere. They are one-stop-does-it-all sorts of places. There's usually a *hypermarché*, a cafeteria, and a gas station. All products and services at these centers will be far cheaper than in town or at regularly advertised highway intervals. Gas in France is outrageously expensive; you'll save if you buy yours from a Commercial Center.

We are big fans of *hypermarchés*, which are found in such centers. Anyone who is interested in retailing will have a ball exploring one or all of these newfangled general stores. Auchan, much like K Mart, is the biggest, but Casino-Géant is the fanciest. You can buy fresh breads, cheeses, and foodstuffs at these markets, make your own picnics, and save a bundle on food. Also stock up on mineral water and Coca-Cola, which are very expensive in your hotel minibar. Most of these *hypermarchés* sell clothes, suitcases, film, and everything else you might need on your stay. So when your friends ask if you've been to the Casino while you were in the South, say yes. Only you have to know it's a supermarket.

Hours

T he South shuts tight for lunch, which means that almost all the stores are closed during this time. Stores open at 10 A.M. and close at 12 P.M. or 12:30; they reopen anywhere between 2 and 3 P.M., or even 3:30, depending on the store. Hours in the South are decidedly relaxed. Stores that stay open throughout lunchtime include the big department stores (there's a Galeries Lafayette in Nice; a Nouvelle Galeries in Menton) and the dime stores like Monoprix and Prisunic, as well as the Commercial Centers. Stores do stay open until 7:30 or 8 P.M. Pharmacies (recognize them by their green cross) open from 9 A.M. to 12 P.M. and from 2 P.M. to 7 P.M.; most pharmacies are closed on Sundays and Monday mornings! Food markets open early and usually dry up by 1 P.M.

Stores that are open Saturday afternoons are closed Monday mornings, and vice versa.

Just about everything is closed on Sundays, including the *hypermarchés*.

The fruit and vegetable market in Cannes is open Sunday (mornings only) and closed Mondays.

Four Days in the South

Please Note: This four-day tour of the South of France was devised to fit the requirements of the Avis Rail N Drive package, which is the cheapest way to see the area, and is timed to bring you to certain cities on market days. Adjust the tour according to your needs.

Day One/Provence:
Aix-en-Provence, Les Baux de Provence, Tarascon, St.-Étienne, and Arles

▾ Take the overnight train from Paris (Gare de Lyon) to Marseille on a Monday night. This gives you a full day in Paris and brings you into Marseille at about 7:30 in the morning on Tuesday.

You can explore Marseille on foot, have breakfast, and then return to the train station for your car. The car is due back exactly twenty-four hours after you pick it up (or seventy-two hours, if you use all the coupons at once), so you can buy yourself some time by taking in Marseille.

▾ Leave the train station and follow the signs for Aix-en-Provence. You'll be taking the A7 and then branching off on the A51; it's all extremely well marked.

▾ Take the exit for Aix Centre and follow the signs to *Centre Ville*. There are specific signs for each hotel once you reach the center of town; we follow the signs to the Hôtel Cézanne, where we check in and drop off the car.

Aix-en-Provence

It's Tuesday, so we're off to the market, which is held in two parts—*brocante* (antiques that are in the garage-sale category) and local specialties (soaps! sachets! herbs!), and then the basic fruit and vegetable market. The core of the whole thing is in front of the Palais de Justice, and stretches from the Place de Verdun to the Place des Pêcheurs, which is the end of the greengrocers' part. This market is held every Tuesday, Thursday, and Saturday from 8 A.M. to 1 P.M.

Although this is our first stop in Provence, we know what we came for, and the market doesn't disappoint. There are tables laden with used bric-a-brac at prices that are better than the prices at similar markets in Paris. But the real buys are from the few vendors who sell handmade and homemade specialties: there are a few soap vendors (prices vary between them, watch out!) and a few vendors selling herbs and bags of the famous dried lavender—which you will find all over the area throughout the day, but not at prices this low. Bargaining is difficult, even out of season. Soap prices throughout the region are within the same range (10–12 francs).

Leave the market by walking into the little *passage* called Passage Agard, which will bring you right onto Cours Mirabeau, the main drag. You may shop the local stores, or take off for the antiques shops (ask your hotel to give you a free brochure listing all the shops, which are mostly clustered in the area around the Palais de Justice or in the Quartier Jaubert, near the city hall). Our plan is to save Aix for later in the day, so we return to the car. But before you admire our self-discipline for not dawdling in Aix, we do confess that there is a Sephora inside the Passage Agard at 12, Rue Fabrot. Prices are a franc or two higher than in Paris, but if you have never been to Sephora, the makeup supermarket, now is your chance to visit.

▼ Back to the car and onto the *péage* A7, the toll road, going through Salon. Exit for the D5 to Les Baux de Provence; there is a green sign that will guide you right to Les Baux, as it is called.

▼ If you're the type who likes to see more and eat less lunch, take a little side trip to St. Rémy de Provence, your first taste of the small villages that offer honey and spice and everything nice. Bypass Les Baux for about 3 kilometers to St. Rémy, where you can smell the lavender-laden air. Circle the town, taking in the two-story redbrick homes, the dark green shutters, the houses with the hand-drawn signs announcing the sale of honey, and the local stores, which all seem to beckon. They are closed for lunch, save Les Olivades, 28 Rue Lafayette, a small shop which sells Gault miniature houses, *provençal* fabric from Les Olivades (a competitor to Souleiado), and home sewing supplies. Take in the Roman ruins, the museum of folk art, and the ice cream and tea shops. Then retrace your steps to Les Baux.

Les Baux de Provence

A medieval city secreted in the rocks on top of a mountain, Les Baux hangs off a winding road that places you above a canyon but is not cantilevered. The city is nestled into the hill in what appear to be caves of rock. The most famous of the hill villages, the town has a population of about 350 people. But they don't get too lonely: About a million tourists a year stop by. So the shopping is pretty good.

Park your car (for which you must pay!) and walk—no cars are allowed. Les Baux is loaded with bistros, cafés, pizza places, and *crêperies*. You'll have no trouble finding a moderately priced lunch. Then explore the city's stores, by walking in the winding alleys—there's a high road and a low road. The most famous shop is La Taste, on Rue de l'Église, which is a chain selling *provençal* herbs and local charm. Many of the stores are decidedly TT's (tourist traps), but manage to attract us, nonetheless. Some of the stores sell local works, which may not be to your taste; many sell *santons*, those small statues of village locals, and tablewares made from *provençal* fabrics. The cheaper version of the *provençal* fabrics is brightly colored; the better-known brands (Souleiado, Les Olivades) not only have more sophisticated colors but more sophisticated combinations of colors. After a half hour in Les Baux you will have memorized everything that is sold in tourist traps, and its price.

▼ Leave Les Baux and head on to Tarascon and the real Souleiado. The road to Tarascon is clearly marked; you can get there on one of two routes—back through St. Rémy or around Les Baux on the D5, where more signs will guide you.

Tarascon

Tarascon has only two attractions for us: a great castle and a fabulous Souleiado shop. This is the factory where Souleiado is made, but sadly there are no factory tours, and the prices here are the same as in Paris.

Like most old cities, Tarascon goes in circles, so you may get lost trying to find the right little street for the estate of Charles Demery, the creative genius behind the Souleiado business. Ask locals if you get lost and keep looking for gates at 39 Rue Proudhon, with a plaque that says plainly: Charles Demery. The Souleiado shop is adorable—it has three chambers decorated to the hilt. High style and romance abound. If you use the bathroom here, note that the hand towel is a large cotton square of their fabric. The front room has the home furnishings and home accessories collection, the middle room has clothes and scarves (and the bathroom), and the farthest room back has fabric on the bolt and remnants (lengths from one to six meters). Even the remnants, which do represent the best buys, are not cheap.

Of the competing brands of fabric, Souleiado is by far the most expensive. The other competitors are careful to keep their prices at exactly the same peg, but Souleiado dares to be bold. They are at least 20% higher than the other brands. Also note that not all Souleiado shops were created equally. The mother shop might be the most fun to look at; the shop in Arles has the best buys and the best promotions. Our homes and our lives are devoted to Souleiado, but stand ready to switch your loyalty to another brand if you want to save some money.

▼ If the Souleiado shop was a disappointment, take the road from town that is marked for, and leads toward, St.-Étienne. As you approach the town, watch for a sign that says "Les Olivades" and points to the right. *Voilà,* there's the factory outlet shop for Les Olivades, with its sign: "Vente au Public." Hours are Monday through Friday, 9 A.M. to 12 P.M. and 2 to 6 P.M. The store has no specific address; this is called the Rue Tarascon, which means simply the road from Tarascon, and you can't go wrong. If you find yourself lost, ask at the church. Les Olivades is famous.

St.-Étienne (Les Olivades Factory Outlet Shop)

▼ If you got into the town of St.-Étienne, you actually went too far. This is a very small village, with a gorgeous church, but shoppers find their religion elsewhere and want to move on. Turn around and watch for the small but plain sign that says "Les Olivades."

You will approach a compound with a stucco villa covered with vines and some new modern buildings and a Quonset hut or two, all painted pale yellow. The shop is a one-room *salon* with a selection of fabrics, sachets, plastic trays, quilted handbags, scarves, etc. *Please note*: The shop accepts cash only! Prices are about

30% less than in stores; once you've shopped here you'll be spoiled forever. Selection depends on how lucky you are. Fabrics may have damages in them; look carefully. These are factory seconds.

▼ Now continue on to Arles, where you'll follows signs to *Centre Ville* and park as close to the top of the Arena as possible.

Arles

Arles has three main retailing areas, all of which you can walk to if you park near the top of the Arena. Stores circle the Arena, stores lead toward the Place de la République, and then stores line the road (Rue Jean Jaurès) all the way to the tourist office on the Boulevard des Lices.

Arles is actually a rather big city, so you want to follow the signs to the city center, pass the old walls (ramparts), and then spot the Arena, which is far more complete than Rome's Colosseum. If you're expecting a lot of Van Gogh retailing you may be disappointed to find a minimum: The tourist office sells a wide selection of postcards in color and in black and white, while a few of the stores in town also sell about a dozen color reproductions in postcard form. The center of retailing is really the Place de la République, which has a few spectacular buildings and many banks, and leads to the Rue Jean Jaurès, a two-block street chockablock with tourist traps and other fun places. The last store on the corner is Souleiado. Check out:

LES OLIVADES: The retail shop whose factory outlet you have already visited on the outskirts. There are a score of Les Olivades shops (hopefully you saw the shop in Paris, so you know the merchandise by now), but this franchise is one of the best. The small shop is crammed with the *provençal* prints in clothes, plastic trays, quilted bags, bolts, and dolls. You'll want it all.

LES OLIVADES, 2 Rue Jean Jaurès

▼

LA BOUTIQUE DU SANTON: It borders on tourist trap, but we don't care. The *santons* are nice, and there are a lot of Van Gogh postcards and a small selection of everything else you might want, from faience to dried lavender. It's worth a look, and a sniff.

LA BOUTIQUE DU SANTON, 1 Rue Jean Jaurès

▼

SOULEIADO: One of the best Souleiado shops we've encountered, because management has risen to the competition and has lots of items available at promotional prices. Maybe we just lucked into a sale last time we were there, but don't rule out Souleiado as too expensive until you've been in this shop. There is a small selection of clothes and accessories, but one wall is totally devoted to bolts of fabric—the store's strong point.

SOULEIADO, 4 Boulevard des Lices

▼

L'ARTISANAT: More local crafts and a large selection of what you've seen in other shops, with a few new twists, including wicker baskets and glass.

L'ARTISANAT, 10 Rue Jean Jaurès

Our favorite store in Arles happens to be back near the Arena, where you parked your car. We like:

LOU BECARU: A fancy tourist trap that sells a good selection of faience and local pottery, some fabrics, and a little of everything else you want. The selection of *santons* is among the best, which is high praise considering that Arles is considered *santon* headquarters. We bought our *crêche* here, and everyone we needed to populate it. Dried lavender is sold in 100-gram bags, for the best price in town. There isn't a real street address here, but don't panic; if you've parked in the city parking area at the top of the Arena you are also at the Théâtre Antique, and this shop is right there, waiting for you.

LOU BECARU, Théâtre Antique

▼ Return to Aix-en-Provence by following signs to Salon or connecting to N113. When you get to Salon you can either get back on the toll road to Aix (well marked) or stay on N113 and enjoy the back-road approach to Aix.

Day Two/Esterel:
La Garde-Freinet, Grimaud, Cogolin, St. Tropez, and Cannes

▼ We're up and out by 8 A.M., saying good-bye to Aix. You can eat breakfast at your hotel, or plan to stop at one of the Commercial Centers on the highway if you want an early start. We'll take the Esterel highway; our goal is to make it to St. Tropez for lunch. The drive is divided into two parts: the easy highway, and then the difficult cross over the mountains and down to the sea. Get on the *péage* A8/E80 toward Nice. The road is very well marked.

▼ Exit the *péage* at Le Luc and then connect to the N7 going to St. Tropez. The connection here takes a little concentration, but it is well marked. Once on the N7, you are on a glorified country road.

La Garde-Freinet

After winding through the gorgeous countryside, you will happen on a small, storybook village that is about halfway to St. Tropez. You can keep on going, which you probably should do if you plan to get to Cannes in time for some heavy-duty shopping; or you may stop and poke around a little bit.

La Garde-Freinet might not be the retailing capital of the Esterel, but it's a good stop to stretch your legs, have a snack, or go to the bathroom. The town is picturesque, boasts a large number of tile and antiques shops, and has a small market in the square. Most of the houses here are made of stone, but a few are covered in stucco—either natural or painted a pastel shade.

Grimaud

Even if you stopped at La Garde-Freinet, you'll want to stop briefly at Grimaud. This can be a quick walk around town to stretch your legs, without even entering a store (perish the thought), but certainly you'll wish to visit this medieval city with its château, church, and memorial to the children who died in World War I. You'll get your first glimpse of the sea from here. Take in the sea, the sky, the vines, and the flowers, and ignore the traffic. If you think you are in heaven, just remember that in a few minutes you will be in Cogolin, where it's market day if it's Wednesday.

Cogolin

Cogolin is only a few kilometers southwest of Grimaud. There are plenty of signs to direct you. Make your way into the new city (actually, village) on the Rue Carnot, which is the main drag through town.

Cogolin is an arts-and-crafts center for the region, and Wednesday is market day. While most of the vendors here will show up in St. Tropez for the Saturday market there, they will also raise their prices a few francs in St. Tropez. Enjoy them as you browse from vendor to vendor. There are fresh flowers galore, tables selling honey, designer dresses from Paris (honest), and sweatshirts for the little ones. Toward the back is a vendor who sells cotton lace curtains by the meter, and our favorite vendor, Marinette, a fabric broker who sells by the bolt. What does he sell that makes us rave? Souleiado (and competing brands, too) at rock-bottom prices! Fabric by the yard can be bought for about half the local retail price. Since the fabric is 1.5 meters wide, you'll want 1.5 meters to make a square tablecloth. Finished tablecloths cost about $100 at Pierre Deux in the United States and at Souleiado in Tarascon. You can do it yourself for about $20.

You can buy herbs—dried or fresh; honey drops; old postcards from the area (blank ones to send to friends) from a vendor who has a box filled with hand-tinted treasures; toys; and more. This is the most refreshing, enchanting market in the area, because it is so natural and unpretentious.

Our salesman from Marinette gave us the local rotation of markets that he visits. If you miss Cogolin on a Wednesday but are staying in the St. Tropez area, any of these markets could be the highlight of your trip:

Tuesday: Lorgues
Wednesday: Cogolin
Thursday: Les Arcs
Friday: Cuers
Saturday: St. Tropez
Sunday: Le Muy

You can park near the town center in Cogolin and walk around the old town (which is slightly elevated) or the main street, Rue Carnot, and the market. It's all rather compact. There are some antiques shops and potteries in the old city. The potteries here sell mostly red clay—unglazed works and not the kind that you will find tomorrow in Vallauris—so wait on pottery. As you leave Cogolin going toward St. Tropez, you'll notice a half-dozen pipe shops—the area is famous for its handmade pipes.

▼ Hit the road (N98) and head for St. Tropez. You are just a few kilometers from St. Tropez, but before you enter town you'll pass a big Commercial Center with a Casino supermarket and many other suburban stores. The entire complex looks very much like a strip center in Southern California, with its sand-colored stucco and red-tiled roofs. If you are considering a picnic on the beach, if you need gas or want to load up on mineral water, now's your chance. Everything in St. Tropez will cost top dollar. Should you need beach things for your kids, there is a Prisunic in St. Tropez—but this Commercial Center will have better prices.

St. Tropez

You can tell we're jaded when we tell you how at home we feel in St. Tropez. After all the years we've lived in Beverly Hills, coming to St. Tropez is like visiting an old friend. St. Tropez is simply the French version of Beverly Hills. You will either loathe it or love it. Certainly, you have to laugh at it. St. Tropez is epitomized by the lady in the Range Rover with the leopard-print silk blouse and the peach suede jacket across her shoulders, her frosted hair held back in a big clip, with her Rolex bracelet watch and her Louis Vuitton tote bag. She squints in the glare, wondering if you took the last parking place or if she will be late for her manicure . . . you're never sure which.

If it's lunch time, shop later (only a few stores right on the waterfront remain open) and eat now. The eateries on the waterfront offer many choices, from a moderately priced pizza to more extravagant dishes from the sea at more extravagant prices. The absolute "in" thing is to sip a drink, or a coffee, or a Coke, or a *café liègois* (there is also a chocolate version—it's a sort of ice cream soda) at Sénéquier, which does not serve food food but is considered the prime spot for watching the world go by. Sit in the red-lacquered beach chairs and stare at the passing promenade. It is a hoot. You can also go to the bathroom at Sénéquier—there's usually a line, but it moves quickly and the facilities are clean. After lunch, you can prowl the town for special little finds.

Shopping in St. Tropez can be broken down into several distinctly different areas. There are many small strips, minimalls, or *passages* built and developed just for the tourist shopper. A large number of vendors come for one season only and are never seen again. Out of season, St. Tropez is pretty slow. In season, it is a mob scene. Certainly the best shopping (to us, anyway) is done at the market in the Place des Lices, each Tuesday and Saturday beginning at 8 A.M. Bring your camera, and all your spare change. If you don't visit on a market day, you'll want to see the Rue du Général Allard, the Place de la Garonne with its Ralph Lauren shop, Kenzo shop, Stephane Kelian, Sonia Rykiel, and other designer spaces; and the waterfront itself, which is mostly cafés but does have L'Herbier, a gourmet food store. There are street vendors crammed into parking spaces along the waterfront, as well. They sell T-shirts and sweatsuits and tourist glitz, which is suddenly something you think you can't live without. Directly behind Sénéquier is a fish market and then a pastry shop (owned by Sénéquier; after 2:30 you can have coffee and pastry while you sit and stare). Then head up to the alleys behind and toward the Rue de la Ponche. (Eat dinner on the terrace of La Ponche, the restaurant.) There's the Rue François Sibilli, which has hot new shops and hopefuls, as well as the established hipsters. You can (and must) walk to Byblos, which is mostly a hotel but is also a nightclub and a sight for sore eyes, with its lavish handpainted interiors and hotsy-totsy boutiques. Certainly the chicest tote bag in the area is the one from Byblos, with their logo printed on it.

▼ Leave St. Tropez on the N98A, in the Cannes direction. The next village you come to, Ste. Maxime, is pleasant but not worth a stop. Hold out for a stop in St. Raphaël, which has a children's amusement park and a Casino-Géant. St. Raphaël seems to stretch on, hugging the coast forever; then you brave the raw rocky roads and see the true Esterel—the red cliffs that fall into the sea. Drive carefully, so you don't.

▼ You will be in La Napoule by late afternoon. You can push on to Cannes immediately, or take a break. We stay in La Napoule at Loew's, so we avoid the Cannes crush. The best idea is to have dinner in Cannes and then window-shop, then return to La Napoule. You can walk. But if you want to do serious shopping, you can go straight to Cannes.

Cannes

Cannes does have an upper city, which is new and much less glamorous than the lower, seaside city, but if you approach from La Napoule, you won't drive through it. The long boulevard along the sea takes on several names as it works its way from La Napoule to the Bay of Cannes, passing the old port and finally becoming La Croisette, the highest-priced part of town, which begins at the Festival Hall, a modern convention center. The lower city has many shopping personalities and several distinct areas:

PROMENADE DE LA CROISETTE

This is the main street in front of the prime part of the beach; it stretches from the Festival Hall to the Carlton Hotel, and then withers away. There are several old grand hotels on this beachfront drive, and many prestigious stores. The most expensive stores, from the boutique Ariane, which carries designer clothes, to the independent designer shops, like Hermès, Gucci, and Cartier, are all located here. The Gray d'Albion Hotel, a modern version of a grand old hotel, hosts a nest of big-name boutiques under its lobby: the boutiques are on street level, the lobby is elevated. You may walk through the *passage* here and connect to Rue d'Antibes for more shopping.

RUE D'ANTIBES

This street is crammed with stores; some of them are designer headquarters for the area, others sell to rich tourists who demand the latest in expensive children's clothes, cosmetics, and ready-to-wear. There are several crystal shops here, where you may find a good price on Baccarat and other big-name French pieces. The many perfumeries are not duty-frees, but they do offer *détaxe* if you spend the minimum required.

RUE HOCHE

This is the back street of Cannes, where the real people shop. There's a Monoprix and a lot of average shops that are fun to browse if you want to see how local people function in a resort town.

RUE MEYNADIER

A small, pedestrian-only area directly behind the old port and in the center of the oldest part of the city, this is the food street you've been anxious to find. Many foodstuffs suppliers here have international reputations (Aux Bon Raviolo; Ceneri), and there is a food market every day except Monday, 8 A.M.–1 P.M.

Finds

LES BOUTIQUES DE GRAY D'ALBION: The space directly beneath the Gray d'Albion hotel houses numerous boutiques, including Hermès, Gucci, and every other big name you can think of. Most of the names here are recognizable, but a few local designers with Côte d'Azur followings are here as well. This is considered the best address in all of Cannes. The area is a useful way of cutting from Promenade de la Croisette to the Rue d'Antibes, since there is a *passage* in between the shopping mall.

LES BOUTIQUES DE GRAY D'ALBION, 38 Rue des Serbes

▼

ARIANE: Right on the beach, but not in the Gray building, Ariane is one of the most famous rich-lady boutiques in the South of France. Stop in for your dose of designer clothes and accessories, local gossip, and beach couture. Ariane is the local representative for Valentino, Missoni, and Escada (exclusively), but there are other names here as well. Great sales in September!

ARIANE, 30 Promenade de la Croisette

CANNES

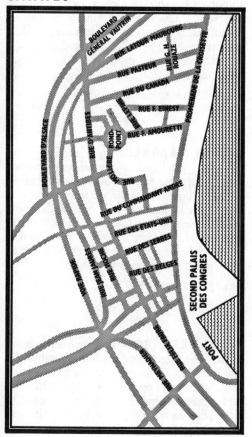

NIL: Cannes is the glitz capital of the area, so it's easy to find costume jewelry at Vanille, a must-see fun shop. But don't miss the smaller Nil, which also has glitz but offers unique pieces, many of which are handmade. Hair ornaments are especially nice, and seem appropriate after a dip in the sea. Prices for the extravagant fun stuff begin at $70.

NIL, 7 Rue de Commandant André

▼

HALLES CAPONE: As you stroll the Rue d'Antibes, you'll see several different designer shops—but don't miss the Marithe and François Girbaud shop, which, like the store in Paris, is named Halle Capone. It is one of the most avant-garde spaces in Cannes, in stark contrast to many of the more traditional shops, but it sells a look that works not only in the South of France, but almost anywhere else.

HALLES CAPONE, 105 Rue d'Antibes

▼

PARFUMERIE RIMAY: There are a number of perfume shops along the Rue d'Antibes: we always return to this one because it has a large selection, it stays open late at night (7:30 P.M.), and it has La Prairie, which can be hard to find. They are not a duty-free, but they do offer *détaxe*.

PARFUMERIE RIMAY, 52 Rue d'Antibes

▼

COMPTOIR SUD PACIFIC: This is the kind of shop we really appreciate—it's different from anything we've ever seen anywhere else. Franchises would probably be very popular in the United States. The company is kind of the Banana Republic of fragrance—you'll get casual and original gifts and fragrances here and find items you haven't seen anywhere else. This is a small French chain that is popular with locals (and in Paris) but is relatively unknown to Americans.

COMPTOIR SUD PACIFIC, 121 Rue d'Antibes

▼

LES PETITS DURS: Trendy kids' shop for rich parents and grandparents who can't resist the urge to buy these wild and delectable fashions. The kind of clothes you imagine the children of movie stars must wear every day.

LES PETITS DURS, 120 Rue d'Antibes

▼

VANILLE: We suggest you pop into Vanille and stock up on everyday glitz. This store carries all the chunky silver and rhinestone jewelry that is so much fun to wear but oh, so expensive in the United States. They also carry a whole line of medallions and earrings for the *faux* military look. Ask them to gift-wrap your package and then let us know, when you get home, how long it took to figure out how to open the bag. We're still working on some of ours. Prices are fair, considering that you are in Cannes.

VANILLE, 4 Rue Commandant André

▼

KARL LAGERFELD: It is difficult to name a designer more prolific and creative than Karl Lagerfeld is today. Not only does he design Chanel and Fendi, but he also has his own line of clothing that he markets with the fan KL logo. Since this has been his personal trademark for so long, we expect that these clothes will be more and more available worldwide.

KARL LAGERFELD, 47 Promenade de la Croisette

▼

NEW ENGLAND COUTURE: This is not a joke! Can you imagine a shop in the South of France specializing in Nina Ricci and called New England Couture? Once you stop shaking your head, you might enjoy popping in. The styles represented are *au courant*, and the prices are the same as in Paris (upstairs, that is). The help is slightly ever so stuffy, but that is probably because they are tired of people asking them where New England fits into couture or the South of France.

NEW ENGLAND COUTURE, 44 Promenade de la Croisette

▼

ALEXANDRA: This is the top boutique in Cannes if you are looking for a large selection of designer lines. It is located a little off the main tourist route, so we think it merits a mention. If you walk away from the Hotel Carlton along the Rue Amouretti, you will come to a funny turnabout called the Rond Point Duboys d'Angers, and Alexandra. Inside you will discover Chanel, Chloé, Montana, and Armani. The selections from each line are carefully made. The only problem, as with most boutiques that carry many lines, is finding small sizes. If you are an 8 to 10 (38 to 40), you are in luck. These are serious designer clothes with serious price tags. No bargains here unless you hit the end-of-season sale.

ALEXANDRA, Rond Point Duboys d'Angers

▼

VIA VENETO: What you can't find at Alexandra you probably can find here. Via Veneto carries Gianfranco Ferré and Thierry Mugler lines of suits in wool and leather at wonderful prices. (That is, they're wonderful if you buy these tony names in the United States; if you think that $100 is all anything should ever cost, you'll find these items high.)

VIA VENETO, 96 Rue d'Antibes

▼

FAUBOURG SAINT HONORÉ: Very often the merchandise is not *au courant*, but it is designer. As a matter of fact, some of the designer merchandise we have seen at Via Veneto we also have seen here . . . just not the same year. It always is worth a look.

FAUBOURG SAINT HONORÉ, 7 Promenade de la Croisette

▼

AU BAMBIN: A delightful stop for picking up everything your kids may need—very dressy to elegant casual. The styles are best in the under-age-twelve lines, with many matching shirts, T-shirts, and pants for both boys and girls. A nice selection of party dresses is available for girls; suits for the guys. The baby clothes are divine. Prices are outrageous.

AU BAMBIN, 84 Rue d'Antibes

Day Three/Côte d'Azur:
Grasse, St. Paul de Vence, Vallauris, Biot, Nice, and Monte Carlo

Do your window-shopping in Cannes before and after dinner, so you're ready to head for the hills. Modify accordingly if you want to stay in Cannes or slow down a bit. If you plan to stay here for a few days, return the Avis rental car and pick it up later, saving your precious coupons for the drive from Cannes to Monte Carlo.

Today's drive is essentially from Loew's to Loew's, with lunch in Nice. If you hate hilly roads, you might want to change your itinerary and do this your own way according to your interests and less rocky roads. Along the coast, you can take in Antibes and Vallauris and have a fabulous time—you'll live without Grasse and St. Paul de Vence. The road to Vallauris is not too steep, whereas the roads to Grasse and St. Paul de Vence are.

▼ Leave Cannes, if you follow our route, and drive through the upper city and follow the signs (N85) to Grasse. This will take you automatically into Mougins. In no time at all, you'll enter Grasse.

Grasse

Grasse is the flower capital of the South, and the place where most of the essences come from for making perfumes and scents. In the old days, all scents were made from floral extracts. Now many of the ingredients are synthetics—perfume manufacturers like synthetics because they offer a wider range of creative possibilities and because they are much harder (if not impossible) to pirate. Indeed, there are only so many flowers and so many combinations. The big thrill in Grasse is to visit the various perfume shops and buy their version of a famous scent.

While Grasse does have a real village with some real-people shops (and lots of big makeup stores), we come here to visit the three major *parfumeries*. In Grasse you are simply asked what your favorite perfume is, and then the similar fragrance is tested for you. For the most part, the three competing shops offer the same things in different packages at more or less the same prices. We prefer Fragonard, mostly because they are the most "American" in their retailing sense and seem to provide the nicest environment for the tour and the testing. But you can have a good time in any of the big three:

FRAGONARD: Not to be confused with the famous painter of the same name, Fragonard is the most famous of the three local *parfumeries*. What they really do is provide essence on a wholesale basis. But they also have two factories, two factory tours, and two factory shops—all ready to seduce you with gift ideas and the possibility of a bargain. Fragrance at Fragonard (as elsewhere here in Grasse) is about 30% less expensive than name brands.

There are four Fragonard locations, two in Grasse, one in Paris (9 Rue Scribe), and one in the nearby hillside village of Èze. Of the two Grasse locations, the new factory—which is slightly outside of Grasse on the road in from Cannes—is more fun. You can't miss it because of all the signs. You can sign up for a tour (in many languages) or go directly downstairs to the shop, which is very large, modern, and bright. The islands in the center display many of the fragrances, the bath salts, the soaps, and other products. The two wall ends are identical and display the perfumes and the *flacons* in which they are sold (unique bottles made to best preserve fragrance). There are fifteen possible combinations of essences.

The most appealing thing about Fragonard is that they are sales-oriented in an American fashion. The plant is modern and a delight to visit; there are well-marked signs on the road directing you to the address; in summer the factory does not close for lunch; they are open 8:30 A.M. to 6 P.M.; and, best of all, they are open on Sundays—so when you want to take a Sunday drive and still get in a little shopping, you've finally found a place that understands you.

FRAGONARD, Route de Cannes or 20 Boulevard Fragonard (Centre Ville), Grasse

▼

GALIMARD: This is the first *parfumerie* on the road into Grasse, with another factory in the center of town. Galimard is sort of the Avis to Fragonard's Hertz. But they just can't try hard enough. Their approach is slightly different in that they trace their twenty-three brands of fragrance to the perfume base families and let you decide which you like. Naturally, if you tell them what famous brand you prefer, they will make suggestions of their own versions. Their packaging for their bath salts is nicer than at Fragonard, but otherwise the store does not compete with Fragonard in terms of the light, airy, *luxe* feeling. They offer a greater variety of candles and soaps than the other shops. The tours are similar.

GALIMARD, Route de Cannes or Place de Gaulle, Grasse

▼

MOLINARD: Molinard has a fragrance sold in U.S. stores called Molinard de Molinard, which you can buy—in many forms—in their store in Grasse. The store is inside the villa, which is gorgeous. There are two rooms, with wooden beams and tile floors and old-fashioned furnishings, which sell various fragrances, creams, candles, and souvenir items. The surroundings inside the shop are more impressive than some of the things for sale, but it is a wonderful atmosphere to visit.

MOLINARD, 60 Boulevard Victor Hugo, Grasse

▼ Back in the car and on to St. Paul de Vence, via Vence on D2210, following signs that say *Nice-Vence*. You will zigzag your way out of Grasse, passing numerous signs that say *Visitez la Parfumerie* as you go.

Vence is the big-sister city to St. Paul de Vence, a tiny medieval city that hasn't had much growth potential in the last 500 years.

▼ Take the D2 and follow the signs to begin the descent to St. Paul de Vence.

You can drive right by St. Paul if you're not careful. Look for signs that say *Centre Ville*, and then immediately look for a parking place— which may be difficult. Cars are prohibited in the actual center of this town built into tiers of rock. Park and walk. With luck you've got cloven feet, or at least good walking shoes, and are ready for a real treat. There really isn't a lot to buy in St. Paul, but it would be a shame to miss this medieval hilltop city.

St. Paul de Vence

Retailing in St. Paul is divided into three levels. On the lowest level, where you have parked, you'll find the most touristy of the shops: there's La Taste; La Collégiale, a general store for all the local kinds of merchandise from Provence and the Côte d'Azur; and a postcard shop that actually sells the last word in status symbols: sweatshirts that say "St. Paul de Vence." Prices in St. Paul are a tad higher than elsewhere.

You can stop at the Café de la Place and watch the old men at their *boules*, or continue up the hill. On the way up there are many opportunities for a coffee, a *crêpe*, or more serious food, should you be interested. There is even a little grocery market (La Ferme) on the next level, so you can buy a piece of fruit or a soft drink in a can.

As you round the steepest corner in France after level two you'll come to Le Ménestrel, for souvenirs, and a few other shops as well as pizza and *crêpe* places; you can walk past the old stone battlements and stare at the architecture or the sea. Curve around to level three, the very top, and then head down, coming out by La Ferme.

▼ Find your car and head down the mountain, backtracking a little bit on the N7 to find Antibes, Vallauris, and Biot. Or connect to the *péage* (A8) and head in the other direction, homing in on Nice. But even if you backtrack we'll get you to Nice for a late lunch, so detour to Vallauris—it's Picasso time, folks, and we bet you're going to spend a pretty franc or so on some of the world's best pottery bargains.

Vallauris

Vallauris is not as cute as many of the villages you have seen in the South of France. It's not even slightly charming. But it has two particular things that make it gorgeous in our eyes: You don't have to fear for your life when you drive, and the savings on pottery and giftables are substantial.

There is a market square, there is a little village, there is a Picasso museum, and there is even a statue of a man and his sheep. Very nice. But what you want before you appreciate all this is the corner of Avenue des Fournas and Avenue des Martyres de la Résistance, so you can begin your two-block stroll through heaven. Check out both sides of the main street (Avenue des Martyres de la Résistance) and then, when you get to Alain Maunier, you'll notice a side street called Rue Georges Clemenceau, which you should then proceed to wander. Many of the stores you just saw on Avenue des Martyres de la Résistance go through the block and come out on Clemenceau, but there are still things to see. We also suggest you enter Les Moulins des Pugets, our favorite store in Vallauris, from the Clemenceau side.

Almost every store on these two blocks is a pottery store, and it continues to amaze us that they can all be so different. Each seems to have its own personality. One shop sells modern works with artistic, monochromatic glazes; another sells paperweights and art glass; another sells unglazed pottery; while yet another has its own patterns of flowers on plates. There are many Picasso-inspired pieces, and there are various styles of ethnic decorating, from the Moorish influence of centuries past, to *provençal*.

Prices in the stores begin at a few francs. For $20 you can buy a decent-sized almost anything—vase, picture, plate—to hand-carry home. All the stores will pack for you; most of them do not ship. Some ship depending on the size of your order. Please note that this pottery breaks and chips very easily; it should not be handled roughly or placed in the dishwasher.

Some of our favorite stops:

TERRE DE PROVENCE: Easily the fanciest store in town, this rust-colored stucco shop is large and stuffed with whiteworks and faience. They have a sign on the door explicitly asking you not to bring in children. Every bit of selling space is crammed with pottery; prices are a little high, but the selection is so immense and the selling process so seductive that you will want to buy everything in the store. Patterns here are extremely traditional; there is nothing funky about this store.

TERRE DE PROVENCE, Avenue des Martyres de la Résistance, Vallauris

▼

LOU PÔELON: More of a touristy store than the others we like, but stocks everything tourists want to buy. Not only are there many styles of pottery here, and many versions of Picasso's roosters, but there are *santons* and Gault miniature houses, in case you missed these items earlier in your trip. There is also a collection called "Naïfs de Karole," which is a group of children that would make a fabulous Christmas collection.

LOU PÔELON, Avenue des Martyres de la Résistance, Vallauris

▼

MUSARRA GABRIEL: This is actually a potter's *atelier* where you can buy from the existing work or commission something of your own. We know several people who have ordered dishes painted to their specifications (the specialty of the house is a monochromatic glaze or a two-color combination) and then sent to the United States. They even had their own initials painted onto the back. This is the last word in style. Extremely sophisticated, and not for everyone.

MUSARRA GABRIEL, Avenue des Martyres de la Résistance, Vallauris

▼

LES MOULINS DES PUGETS: It looks like a dark house that might not even be a store or be open to the public when you approach from the Avenue Clemenceau side, but fear not—heaven is within these doors. The villa has many rooms, since it used to be a mill, and you can wander through them, noting that each is devoted to some other kind of specialty of the area. Buy olive oil from one room, antique glass from another, see the owner's son painting the pottery in the back room, or just stay in the main *salon* and buy everything in sight. Unfortunately this firm will not ship large orders (only small ones), so we did not buy everything we wanted. They wrap in bubble wrap, they gift-wrap, they pack—but they do not ship their sets of dishes or big pottery pieces.

The work here is country style—handpainted nosegays of flowers with ribbon scrolls and borders on white glaze; cherries or olives; bright roosters. The display is fabulous—ceramics and flowers and *provençal* fabrics are all laid out in table settings. We really wept when we saw the toothbrush holders made in the shape of a child (some forty different kids to pick from, all sizes, ages, and colors) that could be laid into the tile of your bathroom at home for a living tribute to your brood. We think the best look is to have one of each pattern of flower on a different bowl and a different plate; then you can buy piecemeal. One of the best gift ideas we've seen anywhere is the soap dish and soap bar combo you can buy—you get a large cake of handmilled soap and a handpainted soap dish for about $14. There are garden pieces in the yard, for those of you who brought the van and have family in the shipping business.

We have never had more fun in a store since we ran out of money at Chanel.

LES MOULINS DES PUGETS, 58 Avenue Georges Clemenceau, Vallauris

▼ With the car filled with pottery, we're off to Biot on the D5 and, yes, we have made a rather crazy circle.

If you can find a better way to see all these places, more power to you. One way to do all this and have more time is to stay in the Cannes area (perhaps the Château du Domaine St.-Martin, an elegant, expensive, and *très mignon* place right in Vence) and do the morning trip that we have just outlined as a full-day trip. This may throw you off on the Avis rental deal if you are planning on getting all the way to Monte Carlo with three driving coupons, but if you are leaving from the airport at Nice and don't care about Monte Carlo, this will be an ideal solution. So think about it. While driving to Biot.

Biot

There are two parts to thoroughly seeing Biot, so don't miss one of them by accident. The well-known La Verrerie de Biot—the glass-making factory with its factory outlet shop—brings a lot of people to the area who follow the signs to the factory and don't realize that the village is perched above it. They see the signs for Nice as they leave the factory, and get back on the road. When the road into Biot branches at the base of the hill on which the city is located, turn left and go into the city and explore. Then come back down and visit the factory as you connect to the road to Nice.

The village of Biot is postcard pretty, with one main street that has the kind of shops that invite you to browse through, even if they do not sell much of anything you haven't already seen or already bought. This is a one-street town, and St. Sebastien is the name of that street. L'Aigurie, 21 Rue St. Sebastien, is a small pottery shop that has a combination of terribly touristy junk and a few real treasures. If you have a good eye, you will enjoy a visit here. L'Ange Verre is down a driveway off the main street, but is worth the few yards' walk, because it is a real-live gallery that sells the most beautiful (and signed) art glass we've seen this side of Kosta-Boda in Sweden. The Maison de Lucille, 36 Rue St. Sebastien, is a small general store selling every touristy item you ever imagined was produced, but there is such a large selection that you may want to spend a few minutes sniffing the air and touching everything. This store has one of the best collections and displays of local soaps you'll see anywhere. Galbe, 28 Rue St. Sebastien, is a snazzier version of a tourist trap, with many items made out of *provençal* fabrics as well as local pottery and glass.

If you really want glass, then do not miss La Verrerie de Biot, which is one of many *verreries* (glassworks) in the area, and the most famous. They advertise heavily; the road into Biot is littered with their hot pink signs and arrows that point the way.

The glassworks has a large parking lot, a snack shop, a souvenir shop, a big observation area where you watch the blowers do their thing, and a large outlet shop. We wish we could rave to you about this place, but we are veterans of the glassworks in Sweden and can tell you, flat out, that this place is for tourists. The prices are outrageously high; there is very little in terms of seconds; this merchandise is nice, and we like it a lot, but once you've paid to ship it—it just might not be worth it. Still, if you like the Country French look, you really don't want to miss this place.

Biot glass is a special kind of glass, filled with tiny bubbles which give it a very country feel. It looks great with faience, with *provençal* fabrics, with American folk arts, or with handmade anything. It's a glass style of the people, but it is very special. The glass comes in many colors, including several blues and shades from rose to burgundy. We like the two-tone pieces. We saw a set of "watermelon" goblets—the cup was burgundy glass and the stem was green. They were beautiful, and the most expensive glasses in the store, we might add.

Besides the shelves and shelves of glasses, there is some faience, some handpainted tablecloths, and a few other items of interest. The shop is very large, with two big rooms devoted to the glass; the third (back) room is actually for shipping, packing, and waiting—there is a long pine bench you can sit on while your packages are being wrapped. In this shipping area is a table or two with broken or second-quality items at lower prices—however, we've never seen anything terrific here. Most of these items are very large and would have to be shipped. You may buy a very tony catalogue. You can arrange for shipping to the United States; it costs an additional 10% for packing and insurance and an additional change per the weight, so expect to add about 25% to the total cost of what you have bought, although you will receive *détaxe*. Because of the weight of the items (with their packing) it is bad judgment to think you will break even on the *détaxe* and shipping. . . . But on small items, you might come out even.

La Verrerie de Biot closes for lunch, is open a half day on Saturday and on Sunday afternoon.

▼ Leave town and follow the signs to Nice. You'll pass Marineland outside of Biot, then connect to the main road at Cagnes. You can either take the *péage* (A8) to Nice (which means you will pay) or the (N7), a pretty good national road that is free. In season, you will find less traffic on the *péage*.

▼ Parking in Nice is difficult; we always go for the lot which is in the center of town right off the Boulevard Jean Jaurès. This allows you to walk to all the shopping areas.

▼ If you're missing American-style mall retailing, stay on the road until right near the Nice Airport (well-marked) and you can hit Cap 3000, which is a zoo of stores and French yuppies—a two-level mall with a *hypermarché* and much, much more. If you like Nice as much as we do, you'll skip the traffic jam and head for the Commercial Center (Cap 3000), and then get out of town. Others may disagree: They find Nice very nice.

Nice

Nice is a large city, crammed with locals and tourists and the big-city hustle-bustle, Côte d'Azur style. Most of the stores are closed during lunch, so stop by for a pizza—Nice is famous for its pizza, called *socca*—or settle down for something more imaginative; you'll have a wait until you get inside the stores. But then, you might just enjoy window-shopping. As you browse, don't miss:

COURS SALEYA

In the upper old town, rather close to the water, this meandering of wide alleys and crooked streets leads to one of our favorite scenes in the South, a flower market. You can eat in any of the cafés that line the way, make your own picnic, or just browse. There are some little shops in between here and there, but mostly this is for browsing and soaking up the charm.

RUE MASSÉNA

This is the best address in town for designer shops and up-and-coming hotshots. Some shops are franchises; they have their own names, while their awnings or windows may have the names of big designers, such as Chanel. Right near the Rue Masséna is the local Promenade des Antiquaires (except on Wednesdays) where locals line the Promenade des Anglais with their wares. The Promenade des Anglais is the street that leads to the famous hotel, the Negresco. If you walk the other way, you'll hit the more commercial part of town. The Place Masséna (where we parked) is a few blocks away; this is more a commercial hub, and hosts the biggest department store in the South, a branch of Galeries Lafayette. The Place Masséna is not particularly charming, but one look at it should not dissuade you from perusing the Rue Masséna. The Rue de la Liberté runs parallel to Rue Masséna and catches the overflow—and the designers who can't quite afford the higher rent on one of the more famous retail streets.

RUE PARADIS

Just a few streets over from Rue Masséna, this is a pedestrian street where the last of the designer shops not on Rue Masséna are located.

AVENUE DE SUEDE

Your last chance to find a designer shop.

▼ Impatient us, we're already onto the *péage* (A8) to Monte Carlo. You can take the N7, the local road, and see a few more villages, but since you've had the afternoon to browse in Nice, you should be ready to get to Monte Carlo before the stores close. Optional stop: tea at Loew's Monte Carlo, 12 Avenue des Spélugues.

When you pull into Loew's, tell them to keep your car handy, as you will need it back shortly. Check in and have a rest stop, then plow through the stores in the hotel. Don't miss the Chinacraft shop, which is outside the front door to the left—it's large and has excellent prices, even when the dollar is bad. If you are not staying at Loew's, get your car after tea and move on to your hotel. If you are staying, drop your stuff and then get up and go. Drive around town checking out the layers of streets and all the shops. You can walk to a lot of places from Loew's, but not everywhere, so take a look-see while you still have the car.

▼ Be sure to take a run by the train station and know how to get there from your hotel. We won't tell you about the hours we spent lost looking for the station. Because you'll be turning in your car rather early the next morning (at the Monaco train station) and hopping on a train just after 9 A.M. (if you continue on our tour, anyway), you'll want to know precisely where you are going!

Monte Carlo

Monte Carlo has added on even more designer shops in the area around Park Palace, but otherwise remains as it has been for the last ten or twenty years: perfect. For such a small place, there is an amazing amount of shopping, so take notice of all these shopping areas:

The *Place de la Casino* is the main square; off it you have the Avenue des Beaux Arts. Between these two areas alone you'll have hit Cartier, Bulgari, Piaget, Christian Dior Furs, Louis Vuitton, and all the other places you go shopping in after you've broken the bank at Monte Carlo.

Avenue Princesse Grace, with its high-rise condos and retail shops in their lobbies, stretches along only about two blocks of beachfront magnificence.

Boulevard Princesse Charlotte is more of a main street up above the water (more stairs!) that runs along the Place de la Casino.

The shopping center Park Palace has lots of good designer shops (Kansai, Krizia, Per Spook) jammed into a small space and also is right off the Place de la Casino.

If you haven't got the look down pat, step into Dimensions, which is an interior-design showroom carrying Manuel Canovas, T. J. Vestor, and Brown Jordan as well as gift items. We did happen to see the single most chic item in the South of France for sale here—a giant tote bag made out of glazed chintz. Dimensions is at 27 Avenue Princesse Grace.

When you've seen enough, return to your hotel for a nap! It's going to be a late night, what with dining continental style, and then a visit to the casinos, and a stroll to window-shop in the area around the Casino de Paris.

▼ If you don't like the notion of a nap and you want to keep on going, how about a short drive to Menton? Take the N7 along the water.

Just two little villages away, Menton is not as picture-perfect as Monte Carlo, but you can have a snack, walk along the beach, or visit the city's main promenade area, which runs perpendicular to the beach (Avenue de Verdun). Be sure to stop at any of the city's major *confiseurs* (candy shops) to get a bag of the local special candy (an almond candy, like marzipan), which is made in the shape of oranges and lemons and green and black olives: all four are bagged together in a melange of color that is pretty to look at and will bring back fond memories of the area. (The sweet is called *les olivettes*.) Menton is famous for its olive wood as well.

Outside of Menton lies the border to Italy. We turn back to Loew's for an evening in Monte Carlo. Italy is tomorrow's adventure!

Day Four/Italian Riviera:
Ventimiglia and San Remo

If you followed our tour day by day, it is now Friday, which is important because this adventure just won't be the same if it isn't Friday or Saturday! If it is Saturday, put more emphasis on San Remo, since it is market day in San Remo. If it's Friday, you can go on to San Remo if you want, or simply spend the day in Ventimiglia before you return to Monte Carlo.

This is a round-trip tour. You should end up back in Monte Carlo to spend the night. Then you can go on to Nice the next day if you are catching a plane, or back into Italy. This is prepared as a day trip, so we assume you are without luggage and are not going on to Genoa.

We also assume you have dropped off the car. If you are on the Avis deal, your three coupons have been used up anyway, and if you take the train you'll be able to avoid driving across borders, finding parking on a market day, or the pressures of driving in Italy. If you are on the Avis deal, please remember that you have a free rail pass, so your ticket to Ventimiglia is free. (You will pay a few dollars more to get to San Remo.)

If you drive across the border, you will pass two sets of border guards, French and Italian. You must show your passport. If you plan to be traveling on to Italy in the coming days and are worried about getting your *détaxe* papers stamped on the train, you may bring your papers and purchases with you and have them stamped now. The train from Monte Carlo to Milan (and other points) will stop in Ventimiglia, and a customs officer should board your train to stamp your papers, but we know from personal experience that they don't always board the trains, and you can be left standing there, high and dry, extremely worried about getting your tax refund.

Ventimiglia

You'll know you're in Italy when you stand in line at the train station and have to clear passport control—in season, this can take a bit of time. Passport control separates EEC passports from others; with an American passport you are an "other." If you have forgotten your passport, forget it. Your Italian shopping spree is on a detour. But since Ventimiglia is just a 40-minute train ride from Monte Carlo, you can still go back and get it. Trains run frequently from Monte Carlo to Ventimiglia. You can arrive on one around 9 A.M. and go on to San Remo during the lunch break. Have lunch in San Remo and then return by a late afternoon train. It is faster to drive, but we like the no-problems aspect of train travel when we are in Italy.

The Ventimiglia market is held a few yards from the train station; just walk right on out. There is a covered fruit and vegetable market, and then, a few yards past, the vendors are out between the palm trees lining the way to the beach selling their goodies. The Louis Vuitton copies are carefully hidden away these days, but this is an Italian market, friends—and never forget it.

The market is large and crowded: beware for your valuables! You'll have to ask for imitation Vuitton, but copies of Gucci, Dior, and Burberry seem to be readily abundant. Prices are not cheap, but run to only about half the price of the real thing in Paris. Best buys are in everyday goods—underwear, sweaters, some leathergoods.

The market closes down around 3:30 P.M., but you should be long gone by then, and on the way to the other end of the scale, for this is our day to travel from the ridiculous (this market) to the sublime: San Remo, with one of the most beautiful Russian Orthodox churches we have ever seen and a street full of designer shops.

▼ Hop the train for San Remo, or drive the A10, the autostrada.

San Remo

In addition to the spectacular church, San Remo boasts Via Matteotti, only a few streets above the waterfront, and is home to designer shops from Benetton to Gucci. Our friend Maggie told us that San Remo had the cheapest Gucci in Italy, but when we last checked it out we discovered that prices were exactly the same as in Rome and Florence.

San Remo has the feel of a resort town—ladies come drenched in fur even into the season. The oldsters hang out at the casino, while the younger set can be seen prowling the designer shops in their too-tight jeans and too-big T-shirts. There are a few outrageously expensive children's clothing shops—perhaps if Grandma breaks the bank at the casino she will buy new clothes for all. Sales help in the big-name shops is surprisingly nice; it is truly a pleasure to shop this Gucci. Almost everything you can buy in San Remo you will later see with greater selection in the big Italian cities, but if you are not going on to Italy—now's your chance to bring home woven leather handbags (Bottega Veneta imitations at half the U.S. Bottega price) and Gucci totes. You won't get the tax refund no matter how much you spend here. So buy your buys and then pack yourself back onto the train headed back to Monte Carlo. Mamma Mia, what a day!

About the Authors

SUZY GERSHMAN is an author and journalist who also writes under her maiden name, Suzy Kalter. She has worked in the fiber and fashion industry since 1969 in both New York and Los Angeles and has held editorial positions at *California Apparel News, Mademoiselle, Gentleman's Quarterly,* and *People* magazine, where she was West Coast Style editor. She hosted a spot on TV's *P.M. Magazine* reporting fashion and trends. She writes regularly for *Travel and Leisure,* and is a member of The Fashion Group in New York. Mrs. Gershman now lives in Connecticut with her husband, author Michael Gershman, and their son. Michael Gershman also contributes to the *Born to Shop* pages.

JUDITH THOMAS was an actress in television commercials as well as on and off Broadway. She left the theater in 1970 to work at Estée Lauder and then Helena Rubinstein. In 1973 she moved to Los Angeles, where she studied for her ASID at UCLA and formed Panache and Associates Inc., a commercial design firm of which she is president. Mrs. Thomas is part owner of a travel agency and is also a consultant to Chapman Evans Co., Inc. She lives in Pennsylvania and California with her husband and two children.